7

D1570198

The Man Who Was
William Shakespeare

The Man Who Was William Shakespeare

Peter Sammartino

Cornwall Books
New York • London • Toronto

Cornwall Books
440 Forsgate Drive
Cranbury, NJ 08512

Cornwall Books
25 Sicilian Avenue
London WC1A 2QH, England

Cornwall Books
P.O. Box 488, Port Credit
Mississauga, Ontario
Canada L5G 4M2

The paper used in this publication meets the requirements
of the American National Standard for Permanence of Paper
for Printed Library Materials Z39.48-1984.

Library of Congress Cataloging-in-Publication Data

Sammartino, Peter, 1904–
  The man who was William Shakespeare / Peter Sammartino.
    p.   cm.
  Includes bibliographical references.
  ISBN 0-8453-4827-2 (alk. paper)
    1. Shakespeare, William, 1564–1616—Authorship—Oxford theory.
  2. Oxford, Edward De Vere, Earl of, 1550–1604.   3. Dramatists,
  English—Early modern, 1500–1700—Biography.   4. England—Nobility—
  Biography.   I. Title.
  PR 2947.09S26   1990
  822.3′3—dc20   89-43010
                                                                      CIP

PRINTED IN THE UNITED STATES OF AMERICA

Contents

Illustrations

The Man Who was
William Shakespeare

1
Why This Book?

What impelled me to write this book? Simply that the question of who wrote Shakespeare's plays and sonnets is probably the most baffling question of Western culture. There have been a number of important and well-written tomes bearing on Edward de Vere, the seventeenth earl of Oxford as the real Shakespeare. All have been meticulously written and are, in fact, legal briefs for the Oxfordian authorship. Necessarily, they have to be very detailed.

I wanted to try to write a greatly simplified version, to serve perhaps as an introduction to the question. Readers can then continue their study of the authorship issue by consulting the more detailed volumes listed at the end of the book and alluded to in the book itself.

I had a further reason to write a book for college students and for high school seniors. Why shouldn't they have a right to know something about the Stratford myth, even though their teachers are wedded through habit to the Shaksper man of Stratford? (I use "Shaksper" to indicate the Stratford man. That, or an approximation, was his name. The pseudonym for Oxford is "Shakespeare" or "Shake-speare.") I have found that young people, if given the opportunity, are fascinated by the question of who was the real Shakespeare. With no vested interests to protect, students are much more open-minded than those whose professional and economic interests are, perforce, cemented to the Stratfordians.

I also had another large group in mind. I have found, as I speak to people in small social groups, that they are fascinated by the Oxfordian case. At first, some of them react with complete disbelief. Of course, Shakespeare wrote the plays. Who else? Why tear down Shakespeare? When I explain that my purpose is not to tear him down but to find out who he was, then most begin to listen. But not all.

Not so long ago, my wife happened to be seated next to a former president of an Ivy League university. She happened to broach the subject of Shakespeare's identity, a natural gambit to open the conversation. The response she received was, "I don't even want to discuss the possibility of anyone but the Stratford man's being the real Shakespeare. If you want to read the real story of why he has to be the author, read the *Literary Supplement* of *The London Times*." I must add, however, that barring this evil topic, the president emeritus was a charming and agreeable conversationalist.

Most people accept without question the Stratford man as the true author of the Shakespearean plays and sonnets. This is what is taught in schools and in the popular books about Shakespeare. It has become almost a religion.

This question of authorship is the greatest detective story of all times. It goes back several hundred years. Some of the issues I hope to illuminate are how the myth started; why it was necessary to create a myth; why it took hold; and why it is so difficult to dislodge it.

Today Stratford in England is certainly the second tourist attraction in the country, next to London. The millions of pounds that pour into England because of Stratford are a strong reason for the continuance of the myth. Can you imagine what would happen to this nicely arranged presentation of the Stratford story if it were established and accepted that the Stratford man was not the real Shakespeare? The effect on the national budget would be sizable; on the Stratford area, the effect would be disastrous.

The other great reason for the preservation of the Stratford myth is that the departments of English in all the universities in the country are committed to it. Can you imagine what would happen to the reputation of thousands of professors if it were established that the true Shakespeare was not the Stratford man? It just wouldn't do to have this happen.

This little book is intended to give the story simply, in abbreviated form, so that the general reader can understand how the myth was created.

Even if a person is convinced that the Stratford man was the real Shakespeare—and most people are in this category—it's good to know what the opposition is thinking.

We, the Oxfordians, give two other reasons for the importance of knowing the contrary arguments. First of all, if we are right (and we fervently think so), then it is immoral to assign credit for writing the plays and sonnets to the wrong man. Secondly, by identifying the earl of Oxford as the real Shakespeare, we can better understand the works in question.

We are not arguing that Shakespeare didn't write the plays and sonnets. We are simply trying to establish who the real Shakespeare was. We are trying to show why it wasn't Shaksper of Stratford.

This is one of the most interesting stories since the beginning of literate world history. In studying the question, we become involved in the true meaning of the Renaissance; in the study of political happenings in Europe; and in the development of literary forms.

Suddenly, the whole world opens up for us. The emergence of England becomes a thrilling story. The brilliance of Elizabeth I, and her stature as a woman of feeling, can be better understood.

After you have read this book, assuming that I have made my points well, reread one of the plays and see if you don't understand it better. Read *Hamlet*, for instance. Since Oxford's mother remarried soon after her husband's death, you can understand Queen Gertrude's reaction. Polonius is Oxford's father-in-law, Lord Burghley. Every author tends to bring his own life into his writing. This is what Oxford did in *Hamlet*.

And now to the most fascinating story in all of literature. Have fun.

It is not easy for a student or any other person to pick up a play by Shakespeare for the first time and really understand it. He or she may get the general idea, but such a play needs reading and rereading, as well as attention to the notes and references by the editor. Unfortunately, all the notes are based on the Stratford authorship.

In many cases, the notes based on the Shaksper assumption do not alter the meaning of the word or expression. But in some cases, the statements are rendered meaningless. For example, Hamlet's statement, "I am mad, north by northwest," is a reference to the fact that the earl of Oxford had invested heavily in the Frobisher attempt to find a northwest passage to Asia. If we have the Stratford man in mind, the phrase eludes any rational meaning.

If one is reading the historical plays, then one needs to know something about the history of the period. Even in certain of the comedies, some knowledge of the play's locale is needed.

Can you get it all when you see it on the stage or in a film for the first time? I don't think so. You may be awed by the scenery, inspired by the acting, impressed by the majesty of the words. But I doubt that most people can really take in all or even an appreciable part of the play.

Shakespeare's plays have to be studied. With each new contact, some aspect becomes more understandable. A friend of mine who was a symphony director said that he read a symphony twenty-seven times before attempting to hear it or direct it. A Shakespearean play is like a symphony. It has to be read, studied, read again and again, and explained; only then might one get a full appreciation of the work of art. Even then, there will be words or phrases that will remain beyond understanding. Some words or expressions have changed in meaning over the centuries. In some cases, a word may be mangled because of a blot of ink on the imperfect copies that were used in the First Folio, for, no original manuscripts were available when this project to bring out the plays was attempted.

If the Stratford man is kept in mind, Shakespeare's works are even more difficult to understand. If instead you reason that the writer was the earl of Oxford, the plays and sonnets become ever so much clearer. As I've already said, this is the greatest detective story in history, taking place in one of the most interesting periods in history. It was a period when the greatest empire at that time, Spain, began to lose importance. At the same time a relatively small country, England, second in importance to both Spain and France, began to achieve world greatness. Arising out of a depressed cultural standing, England took inspiration from the Renaissance movement that was being developed in the various Italian states. And who should be the prime mover in this inspiring transformation?—Edward de Vere, the seventeenth earl of Oxford, who wrote anonymously at first, but then was forced to adopt a pseudonym—Shakespeare—(or Shake-speare).

Even those who have locked themselves into the Stratford mold might try assuming that the writer of the plays and sonnets was the earl of Oxford. I guarantee that the exercise will help them to appreciate his works.

A book such as this cannot really be read in one sitting. Each chapter must be read independently. It is almost as if each could stand as a separate article. Therefore it becomes necessary, if my position is correct, to repeat certain facts and events in order to make the thinking clear within the chapter.

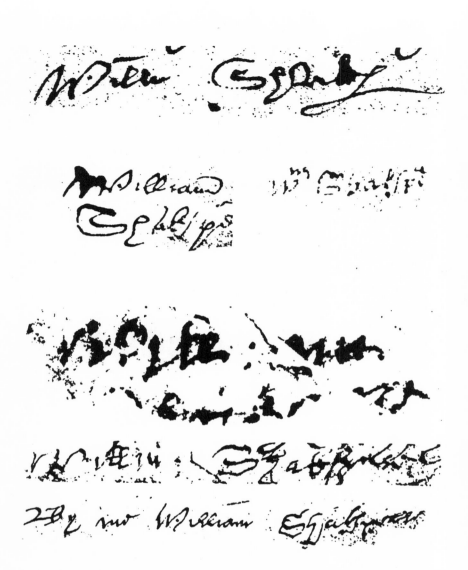

Signatures. This is all we have of the writings of Shaksper of Stratford—six almost illegible scrawls.

2
Shaksper of Stratford

The whole Stratfordian case is built on the life of William Shaksper of Stratford. To begin with, his name was never William Shakespeare. It was variously Shaksper, Shakspere, Shaqsper, or Shaxpere. The emphasis was always on the first syllable, pronounced with a short a.

The only handwriting we have of his is that of six signatures, three of which are on his will. Of various spellings, they look like the scrawls of an illiterate person. Moreover, it would seem as if someone were directing the writer's hand. One signature seems made up of two parts, one is a scrawl, and the rest bear a different calligraphy, which would indicate that someone else completed the name. And that's it: not a single letter; not a single note; not a single piece of writing other than the signatures.

But let's go back a few steps and examine what we know of Shaksper and his family. For we do have facts about him. The only trouble is that the facts we have do not relate in any way to a writing career.

Let's start with Shaksper's father. The earliest fact known is that in 1551 he was fined for having a dunghill in front of his home in Stratford. In 1557, he married a Mary Arden of the town of Wilmcote. Four years later he was elected as what we would consider a councilman of the borough. In the town of Stratford, only six of the nineteen officials could write their names. Thirteen could not read or write.

We don't know exactly when son William was born, but we do know that he was baptized on 26 April 1564. Mark that year well, because it will be an important fact in the case against Shaksper. By that time, the earl of Oxford had already received his first college degree from Cambridge. When the tour guide in Stratford points out where Shaksper was born, he or she is making an incorrect statement. We don't know where he was born. An attempt was made to correct this statement, but the request was brushed aside because the body that made it was declared not legal. It was a pure bureaucratic runaround.

In 1571, we have another fact. William's father sued to collect a debt of fifty pounds from the son of an old friend. From the next year on, his father's involvement in borough affairs began to wind down. As a matter of fact, in 1573 he was sued for a debt of thirty pounds and issued an arrest warrant.

In 1577, the financial condition of the family deteriorated. The father had to mortgage the house that his wife had inherited. Furthermore, he no longer attended borough meetings. By 1579 he was unable to pay the town levies—the equivalent, more or less, of a special tax. The following year he was brought up on charges of disturbing the peace and fined twenty pounds, which was a sizable fine at that time. He also reneged on the payment of a forty-pound debt and, as a result, lost the house that his wife owned. This about winds up all the facts concerning William's father. There is not a word about schooling or any intellectual activity of any kind.

The matter of school in Stratford is one of the mysterious questions that has come up. We must remember that Stratford was a small, unimportant town. There probably was a primary school of sorts. It might have been a one-room affair with a single, so-called hornbook for the pupils to use. But to be admitted, a boy or girl would still be required to know how to read and write. Also, some expense would be involved. There are no town records that indicate the municipal support of a school. Shaksper reached primary-school age during the very period in which his father's financial position was deteriorating. Moreover, who would teach young Shaksper to read and write? His parents were illiterate!

Now, if the school were of a higher grade, then there would have been some record of it. Surely, some of the students, either in town or elsewhere, would have been mentioned. In fact no one in town, and for several generations, ever alluded to an important school. This idea of Shaksper going to school appears to have been made up out of whole cloth.

The next thing we know is that on 27 November 1582, young William who was then eighteen years old, took out a license to marry Anne Whately. The name used is Willelmum Shaxpere.

But the next day, the marriage bond names not Anne Whately but Anne Hathaway whom he had gotten pregnant. She is eight years older than he is. On 26 May 1583, a daughter Susanna is born. The reason for the change is obvious: he couldn't marry Anne Whately because Anne Hathaway was pregnant.

By this time, the earl of Oxford had been pursuing a full dramatic and literary career. He had written early versions of later plays for court presentations. He had traveled to Italy. *Love's Labour's Lost* was being turned out, and he had acquired a lease on the Blackfriar's Theatre. Most important, his company of players, on tour through the provinces, performed at Stratford. Could this be when the earl of Oxford and Shaksper met? Possibly. But still we have few facts regarding the Stratford Shaksper. On 2 February 1585, his twins, Hamnet and Judeth, were baptized. Hamnet died in 1596. We have said in passing, that his parents were illiterate. So, evidently, were his two daughters!

By 1590, some of Shakespeare's plays were coming out anonymously in completed form (all experts assume, although we actually don't know what the finished products were really like). But nothing is known about Shaksper during all these years. If you read in any of the Shakespeare biographies that the Stratford Shaksper was doing this or that, it is simply made up. I repeat, nothing is known about the Shaksper man during those years.

Aha! All of a sudden, in 1597, the Stratford man bought New Place, the second-best house in Stratford. The next year he was cited for hoarding grain during a famine. He is listed as a tax delinquent in London, so he must have been there before this date. The date of Shaksper's arrival in London is an elusive one, both for Stratfordians and for Oxfordians. It could be as early as 1586 or as late as 1596.

Possibly before 1596 William's father applied for a grant of a coat-of-arms. Such a grant had to be approved by the Queen's Heralds, as is the custom to this very day. The application was turned down. The notation on the application is "non, sanz droict," meaning, "no, the applicant has no right."

But in 1596, the comma disappeared. Now the words of the turndown read "not without right" and are adopted as the motto of the arms. This time the grant was approved. Ben Jonson, in his play *Every Man Out of His Humor*, indicates that it was bought, and he even makes fun of it by giving his character the motto

"Not Without Mustard." This grant of the coat-of-arms is blown up by the Stratfordians to indicate that Shaksper was really a nobleman and therefore privy to the happenings of the Court. Nonsense!

In 1602, Shaksper bought a second house. In July 1604, a Willielmus Shexpere sues an apothecary in town to collect a loan made three months before. In July of that same year, he purchases tithes in Stratford for £440.

In 1607, his daughter married a John Hall. Her name is entered as Susanna Shaxpere. Shaksper (this time his name is spelled Shackspeare) again sued a fellow townsman for the collection of a debt. In 1614, he collected from the town of Stratford a minor sum for having supplied two quarts of wine served to a preacher. In the same year, a "Shackespeare" was involved with others in the illegal enclosure of common lands in the village.

In 1616, he made the will bearing the almost illegible signatures, and in April of that year, he dies as "Will Shakspere, gent."

What do you notice about all the things we do know about the Stratford Shaksper? Were any of them of literary consequence? No!

Do we have a single indication, either in Stratford or in London, that he wrote anything? No!

Bearing in mind the chasm between nobility and the common people, do we have any indication that he was in any way connected to the court? No!

Is it possible that Shaksper, who was avid for any penny, would never pursue his commercial interest in plays? No!

Do we have any indication that the Stratford man, apparently interested in the coarser aspects of a town's commercial activities, had the sensitive, courtly, and romantic sensibilities of Shakespeare? No!

But, you say, in the books on the Stratford man a complete life for him is described, detail for detail. My reply is that all these filled-in details are made up, assumed, and simply concocted to fit the Stratford myth. I have given the facts as we know them. Everything else is fictitious.

Well, what about the monument in Stratford? That was part of the plot that will be explained in a later chapter. It is not known who put the monument there, but it was certainly no one from his family. The idea was to plant "evidence" for the Stratford man. The first design showed his hands resting on a sack of grain. This didn't show that he was a writer, however, so the sack of grain became a pillow, and a quill pen was put in the man's hand. The monument doesn't really bear any evidence he is an author. The poem is pure doggerel. It is stated that the body lies within the monument. In fact, the body is elsewhere, and anyway, the monument is too small to contain it. The whole arrangement is a clever plan. To the people of Stratford, it was simply a monument to someone who made money. To outsiders who believe in the Stratford myth, it represents a fitting monument to a literary legend.

The ploy of the Stratford believers is to diminish the extent of Shakespeare's knowledge while exaggerating the educational background of Shaksper. This is designed to make the myth more plausible. If the case still sounds unconvincing, then they fall back on the statement, "Oh, but he was a genius!"

The matter of dates is basic. The dates given for Shaksper's London activity have been artificially antedated to give the Stratford story credence. With the earl of Oxford, there is no need to manufacture any dates. Every fact holds up naturally. The plot to strip Oxford of his authorship and to create someone else who would be given the credit is perhaps understandable. Nevertheless, it is evident that only the earl of Oxford could have written the plays and sonnets of Shakespeare. In fact, many Shakespeare plays appeared before Shaksper could possibly have written them.

One last word: If Shaksper had written all the plays, wouldn't he have been in some way involved in the preparation and plans for the First Folio? Yet there is no evidence that he was remotely involved with it during the long years before its issuance.

Lord Burghley. The father-in-law of the earl of Oxford. (By permission of the National Portrait Gallery, London.)

3
How the Myth Got Started

How did the myth get started? You must remember that Shaksper didn't get any attention in Stratford while living and for many years after his death. No one in Stratford, as far as we know, spoke of him as a writer, nor for that matter as a known actor. On the other hand, in London, any accessible records of the earl of Oxford would have been expunged by his father-in-law, Lord Burghley.

In 1681, John Aubrey created the supposed life of Shakespeare. He stated that the author had a most prodigious wit, that he had been a schoolmaster, and that he lived in Stratford.

In 1709, Nicholas Rowe published an edition of Shakespeare's plays and wrote a biography of the author.

Both biographies improvised, but this much is apparent: The Stratford man's life was in no way related to the rich tapestry of material in the plays or sonnets. Further, there is not a shred of evidence that he was ever interested in preserving any of the plays or poetry.

In 1769, there was a Stratford jubilee. Some fellows from the chamber of commerce were whooping it up. One of them, David Garrick, implied that the local boy William Shaksper had been a great writer. The Stratford attribution had begun. It didn't make sense. There were no tangible facts to support it. But somehow the myth got started. Anything to put Stratford on the map! And so began the movement that Henry James called, "the biggest and most successful fraud ever practiced on a patient world."

In an 1837 novel, Benjamin Disraeli, wrote, "And who is Shakespeare? We know of him as much as we do of Homer. . . . Did he write a single whole play? I doubt it." He was, of course, referring to the by then popularly accepted Stratford Shaksper.

There were voices of disbelief from many sources. How could this illiterate Stratfordian have written such plays and poems! By

1940, a professor at Northwestern University listed more than 4,500 articles and books that questioned the Stratford authorship. Whitman, Whittier, Henry James, and Mark Twain all came out against the Stratford man. Mark Twain said, "He [the Stratford man] hadn't any history to record."

Shaksper was born in 1564. If we can assume that a writer does not achieve maturity until he has passed twenty-five years or so, Shaksper would not have been able to start on his major works until around 1590. But Shakespeare refers to events that took place in 1578 in the courts of France and England indicating that he was near to sources of power.

Perhaps we should bring in at this point a few words about the Folger Shakespeare Library in Washington, D.C., a nonprofit institution established by Henry Clay Folger in 1932 and administered by the trustees of Amherst College. While it is supposed to be dedicated to the objective study of Shakespeare, it seems to be committed to the Stratford point of view and has belittled any efforts to question the Shakesparean orthodoxy. Recently, however, it has proclaimed that it is open to any research that bears on the Shakespeare question.

Charles W. Barrell, a noted Shakespeare researcher, succeeded in making an infrared X-ray photo of the Shakespeare portrait in the Folger Gallery. He found that it was a painted-over portrait of the earl of Oxford.

When the Barrell photographs were publicized, someone asked Dr. Giles Dawson, acting for the Folger Library, for his comments. Dr. Dawson replied, " . . . they must have been doctored up." Barrell sued Dr. Dawson. At the trial, Dawson, under oath, admitted that he could not give a single fact to support the supposition that Shakesper was the author of the Shakespearean plays—not one. The case was settled out of court, but Dawson made a public apology. He acknowledged that the Folger Library had made an independent examination of the paintings after the Barrell examination but had never publicized the findings. Apparently, its examination confirmed that of Barrell.

The original painting has since been alleged to be that of another noble. I still believe Barrell's findings, however. He was a meticulous reseacher, careful in his methodology and conservative in his assumptions. He passed away before the new

Folger findings came out. Now everyone seems to have forgotten the whole matter. But one important fact remains: Under oath, an outstanding Stratfordian couldn't cite a single fact to uphold the Stratford position. Incidentally, the lawyer for Barrell was Charlton Ogburn, Sr. who, with his wife, Dorothy, wrote that classic, *This Star of England.* Also, the controversial painting is still exhibited as a portrait of "William Shakespeare," presumably the Shaksper person.

Mind you, for hundreds of years orthodox scholars have been hunting for traces of information about the Stratford man; yet in 1949, a Stratford expert could not cite a single fact that could support the Stratford theory. Walt Whitman was to state that on the Stratford man "the record is almost a blank—it has no substance whatsoever."

Of the things we do know about the Stratford Shaksper not a single one is connected with writing or acting or literature. We don't know exactly when or where he was born, despite the lies that tourists to Stratford are fed regarding these two matters. British literary columnist Bernard Levin refers to such statements as "monumental frauds."

Shaksper must have gone to London at some time, but there is no evidence as to the exact year. I think it may have been around 1590.

Shaksper is supposed to have held shares in two London theaters, but curiously, in his will, there is no mention of such ownership. One would think that a man who was careful to list every item of furniture would be especially careful to list a major asset such as ownership in theaters.

These minor happenings are important because they make us wonder how, in 1597, Shaksper could buy "New Place," the second-largest house in Stratford. Where did he suddenly get so much money? Some Stratfordians say that he made the money selling his plays. But this is fallacious. We know that other playwrights didn't make one tenth of what was involved in Shaksper's apparent new income. The inevitable conclusion is that he must have been paid off for something. All his commercial or real estate operations are an open book. They are not, however, a reason for his sudden wealth.

Shaksper of Stratford was paid off for something. What could he have been paid off for? The only rational explanation is that he served to disassociate the earl of Oxford from the writing of plays that revealed too much of Court happenings. Thus the authorship was transferred from the nobleman Oxford to the commoner Shaksper. The payment had to be large enough for the commoner to be willing to take the chance. After all, John Stubbs had lost his right hand because he, in a pamphlet, had opposed the queen's marriage to the French duke of Alençon.

Another case might be cited here to show the heavy censorship that prevailed. In 1597, the playwright Thomas Nashe wrote a play, *Isle of the Dogs*, which was found to have seditious material. Nashe was clapped into jail, his theater was closed, and all existing copies of his play were destroyed. We have, therefore, two strong reasons why the earl of Oxford had to hide his writings: (1) it was the unwritten rule that noblemen could not attach their names to published plays or poetry; and (2) for state reasons, a heavy censorship operated.

The claim is made that Shaksper was an actor—and a well-known actor at that. But here again, patient research fails to bring forth any supporting evidence. A study of the records of all the towns in which acting companies appeared for the period reveals no mention of William Shakespeare. Neither does a study of payments to actors in the theaters of London at the time.

Stratfordians claim that Shaksper's genius allowed him to learn how to write quickly; that he either mysteriously acquired all the thousands of facts and allusions in his plays or that he had numerous friends in court and in London to feed him all these facts. Stratfordians conveniently forget or fail to mention that Stratford was a small town of exactly 171 houses. The local dialect was so unintelligible to Londoners that when Stratford recruits were brought to the capital for the preparation for the Spanish Armada, interpreters were required.

Most people assume that Shakespeare and Shaksper are one and the same man. But the facts clearly indicate that "Shakespeare" is a pseudonym. Nearly half of the time it appears not as "Shakespeare" but as "Shake-speare," a form that in itself suggests that the name is a nom de plume. Fifteen of the thirty-two editions of Shakespeare plays published before the 1623 First Folio naming the author bore the hyphenated name! Evidently Oxford, who had been writing his plays anonymously, had come to the point where he had to decide on a name. The name

Shakespeare was a natural choice. One of his titles was "Lord Bulbeck," whose coat-of-arms includes a spear. Also, Gabriel Harvey, a Trinity College Fellow, referred to Oxford in a speech, saying, "Thy countenance shakes a spear." Oxford was a major participant in court tourneys presented before Queen Elizabeth, and thus was outstanding in "shaking spears."

The name "Shakespeare" was first used in 1593 with the publication of the long poem *Venus and Adonis*. Incidentally, Venus really alludes to Queen Elizabeth; Adonis is the earl of Oxford. The name "Shakespeare" appears not on the title page but only in the dedication, which includes the phrase "the first heir of my invention." This clearly indicates that the name is a pseudonym. A year later, *The Rape of Lucrece* appeared, also with the dedication signed "William Shakespeare."

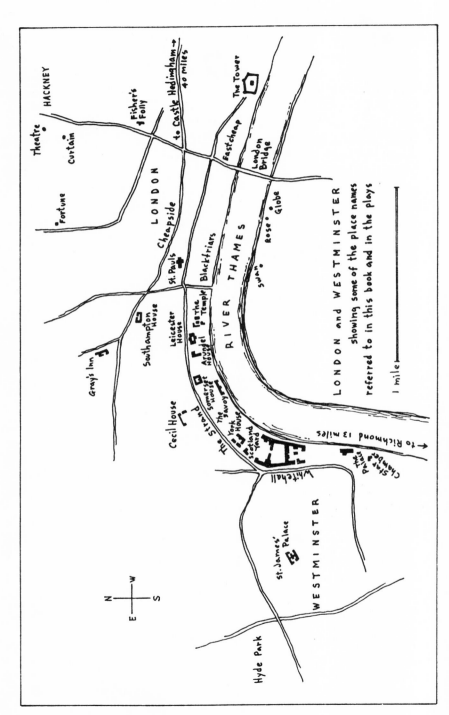

London. Showing places referred to in this book and in the plays of Shakespeare.

4
The Political Situation in Europe

In the effort to understand the plays of Shakespeare, it is helpful to review two historical matters: (1) the political situation in Europe at the time of Queen Elizabeth I, and (2) the earl of Oxford's trip to Italy in 1575 and 1576. The latter we shall take up in a separate chapter.

During the reign of Queen Elizabeth I, there were four main political powers in Europe: Spain, France, England, and the Netherlands. For our purposes, we need not concern ourselves with Austria, Russia, or the various states of Italy, although the Pope did influence the religious happenings in England.

Spain was absolutely Roman Catholic. So too, had England been Catholic until Henry VIII cut it away from Rome. Edward VII, who succeeded Henry VIII, strengthened Protestantism within the country. He was succeeded by Queen Mary I, who reversed the process, and England became mostly Catholic.

Queen Elizabeth, who succeeded Mary, returned England to the Anglo-Catholic Church. The change was a political one, however. The majority of the nobles had Catholic leanings. This state of affairs was to play an important part in the life of the earl of Oxford, who was primarily skeptical but a Catholic in spirit, although his loyalty to the country and to Queen Elizabeth came first.

In France, there were two religious factions: the Catholics and the Protestants (Huguenots). The rulers were Catholic, but there existed a strong religious opposition. As part of a continual struggle between the two groups, in 1572 there was the massacre of St. Bartholomew's Day, when top Huguenots and their followers were murdered en masse. This brought about a revulsion in Queen Elizabeth and was to affect deeply her attitude toward Catholic plotting.

In the Netherlands, the situation was complicated. It was technically a part of Spain. Philip II of Spain was determined to make the country thoroughly Catholic. The English, equally determined to strengthen Protestantism, provided covert help to the Netherlands—a strategy not too different from that used today by the United States and Russia in various parts of the world.

Spain at the time was the most powerful empire in the world, and Philip II was determined to make it even stronger. His empire included the Netherlands; southern Italy, including Sicily, and Milan; Portugal; Mexico; the West Indies, and large portions of South America. The only power that stood in his way was England. One of his plans was to have Spanish troops in Flanders cross over and attack England. Queen Elizabeth, trying to keep her country on an even keel, was careful not to provoke either Spain or France into war. Her covert assistance to the Netherlands' William of Orange, however, had turned open by the 1580s.

In Scotland, Mary, Queen of Scots, a relative of Elizabeth, ruled as a Catholic. So there were the Catholics (Spain, France and Scotland) and the Papal States on one side, and the Protestants (England and the Netherlands,) and the Huguenots (France) on the other side. It was conflict in France that eventually led many Huguenots, seeking religious freedom, to come to America.

Queen Elizabeth faced divisiveness among her own people: the Catholics wanted to install Mary as queen of England. This conflict was reflected in the life of the earl of Oxford.

To give you one example of how these political events dovetailed into the life of Oxford, and how they came into his plays, let us take the example of *Titus Andronicus*. Oxford had told Queen Elizabeth that one of the nobles, Arundel, was plotting against her. Arundel, in order to buy time, made countercharges against Oxford, all imaginary. Oxford's accusation turned out to be true. Arundel was plotting with Philip II of Spain to bring Mary, Queen of Scots, to replace Elizabeth as queen of England. In the play, the character Aaron, which is also the title of the first part of *Arundel*, portrays the conspirator. This was an early historical play in the series that Oxford wrote to help Queen Elizabeth consolidate the support of the English people in the covert struggle against Spain. The play is bloody, vicious, murderous, horrendous. He was depicting the horror of the massacre in Antwerp, perpetrated by the Spanish and known as the Spanish Fury. Here we have a succinct example of how the plays, under the pseudonym "Shakespeare" or "Shake-speare," fit in with the life of the earl of Oxford. It is impossible that Shaksper of Stratford, without any education, could have written by chance verses that contained so many references to the activities of Oxford. (More important, as a commoner, Shaksper would have sought a patron to dedicate the plays to, in order to secure financial support.)

Let us return to the actual history, and talk about Queen Elizabeth. Philip II made overtures to her. Spain and France, while they were both Catholic, were enemies nonetheless. It made sense for him to "get along" with England, in the sense of taking over the country quietly, without the expense of war. Queen Elizabeth, trying hard not to offend him, spurned his advances.

Meanwhile, in France, the Queen Mother, Catherine de Medici, was also trying to effect an alliance with England. She sent over one of her sons, Alençon, who paid court to Elizabeth. Alençon was short, pockmarked, and young enough to be her son. Elizabeth, again trying not to offend a foreign nation, behaved coolly, calling him "my frog." Although she seriously considered a match for political reasons, she eventually turned him down.

Elizabeth was an outstanding woman of her age. Utterly devoted to serving the interests of her country, she was well-educated and steeped in classical studies. Nevertheless, being the daughter of Henry VIII, she had human yearnings. She undoubtedly had secret lovers, one being the earl of Oxford, even though he was seventeen years her junior.

I am convinced that she bore him a son who was conveniently made a changeling for the duchess of Southampton and was known in history as Henry Wriothesley, earl of Southampton. But this assumption need not interfere with the Oxfordian thesis. Until new documents are discovered, we can only guess who the mother of the "fair youth" of the sonnets was. That Oxford had an illegitimate son is fairly certain, as evinced in the sonnets. Whether it was Queen Elizabeth's or some other woman's is at present a mystery.

Queen Elizabeth was an imperious woman and didn't like her lovers to become involved with other women. When the earl of Oxford took as his mistress one of the ladies-in-court, Anne

Vavasor, and gave her a son, Elizabeth had both thrown into the Tower. When her favored suitor, Leicester, married the countess of Exeter, Queen Elizabeth was extremely rude to the wife, once slapping her face in public.

Do read more about Elizabeth. She was one of the great women in history. More important, knowledge of her life will explain much about the Elizabethan era, or shall we say, the Shakespearean era.

At this point, let us go over the religious makeup of the English nation. In Elizabethan England, one might discern three groups:

1. The Roman Catholics who desired to continue a relationship with the pope, the vicar of Christ.

2. The Puritans, who favored a close application of strict European Protestantism. A simplification of the role of the Puritans at the time of Queen Elizabeth was that they represented a more thorough reformation than that represented by the Church of England. This stance was inspired by the Calvinistic teachings emanating from Switzerland.

3. The Anglicans (Church of England), who, while eschewing monasticism and welcoming the use of English in its services, did not favor the strict Calvinistic interpretation, rejected all foreign liaison, and felt that ecclesiastic government should come from the sovereign. Queen Elizabeth, like her father, Henry VIII, favored this position.

What really concerns us in this volume is that the earl of Oxford was closer to the group having Catholic leanings, until he realized the treasonable ends they had in mind. At that point, loyal to Queen Elizabeth and his country, he turned against the conspirators and laid bare their plans to the queen. Oxford turned to the French ambassador who was present to corroborate his accusations. Unfortunately for Oxford, the foreign diplomat, in order not to get involved, disclaimed any knowledge of the treasonable machinations on the part of Arundel and Howard, another conspirator. Oxford was left in the lurch. Later, as we have said, all his accusations turned out to be true.

A word should be said about recusants—Roman Catholics and even Puritans who refused to attend the services of the Church of

England. According to the rather fickle laws of the period, such a person could be fined, lose his position, or even put in jail. It was this forced observance of the Anglican practices that led eventually to the emigration of Puritans to found a new colony in a new country.

It is impossible to understand the political climate of that period without understanding the concurrent religious pressures. To this day, we have religious pressures—of a different sort to be sure, but tragic nonetheless. The conflicts in Iran, Israel, and India serve as examples. Freedom of religion is not an easily accepted doctrine, and it was the determination to guarantee this freedom that led to its incorporation into our own constitution.

England as we know it really started when the Norman conquerers arrived in England in 1066; from then on, one king succeeded another. England had kingly rulers before the Normans, however. But when the Normans took over, all other dynasties were abolished. Was the line of succession always from father to son? No. Sometimes when there was no son or daughter, some other branch of the family got into the line of succession. And sometimes there was a rebellion, such as that of Bolingbroke against Richard II, resulting in Bolingbroke's reign as Henry IV.

You do need a minimal knowledge of English history of the period in order to understand the Shakespearean chronicle plays. Sometimes changes take place because some one person becomes powerful enough to seek the leadership. Usually, however, economic conditions force a change to take place. The growing strength of Parliament plays a role, too, but Parliament grows stronger when the sovereign has minimal resources and must beg the House of Commons to legalize more taxes.

You will hear that Oxford was a Lancastrian in his sympathies. What does that mean? Simply that, at one time, there were two branches of the royal family that were vying for power: the Lancastrian branch and the House of York. During the reigns of Henry IV, who belonged to the House of Lancaster, and Henry V, there was relative peace. When the latter died, however, the crown went to Henry VI, a nine-month-old child who grew up to be weak physically and mentally. There was economic distress and excessive taxation. The country was also in disarray because it had lost most of its possessions on the continent.

Civil war erupted in 1455, and the so-called War of Roses

(Lancaster branch versus the York branch) lasted thirty years, ending with the defeat and death of Richard III at Bosworth Field in 1485. The Lancastrian Henry VII united both branches by marrying Elizabeth (not the one in our story), the York heiress.

He was succeeded by Henry VIII, the king of many wives. The important thing to remember about Henry VIII is that he freed England from its chains to the pope by divorcing his wife Catherine and marrying Anne Boleyn, mother of Queen Elizabeth I. Henry VIII was succeeded by Edward VI, the son of his third wife, Jane Seymour, and then by Mary I, his daughter by his first wife, Catherine of Aragon. Mary I returned England to Roman Catholicism, reinstituting the Mass and reestablishing the authority of the pope. She also restored the church lands, thereby impoverishing her country. She married Philip (later Philip II) of Spain, who embroiled her in a disastrous war against France.

Mary I was succeeded in 1553 by Elizabeth I, daughter of Anne Boleyn and Henry VIII. This is the regime that concerns us directly in the story of the earl of Oxford.

Elizabeth had received a thorough classical education and knew Latin, Greek, French, and Italian. She assumed the crown when her small country was nearly bankrupt and was one of the less powerful European nations. When she died, however, England was leading all the others and was on its way to become the largest colonial empire in the world.

She steered the country back into Protestantism. Helped by good counselors—Burghley, Walsingham, and Leicester—she followed a path of relative peace and economic development.

While she sought good advice, she did not let any one man or clique manipulate her. She cleverly played off one enemy against another—France against Spain, for example. She managed to keep England secure and to ward off foreign interference.

Despite her insistence on complete subservience to the service of her country, she was also a woman and had a series of favorite suitors—Sir Christopher Hatton; earl of Oxford; the earl of Leicester, whom she considered marrying; the earl of Essex; and Raleigh. Unfortunately, Essex was found guilty of treason and had to be executed.) For diplomatic reasons, as we have mentioned, she also toyed with the idea of marrying the French duke of Alençon.

She was frugal, but who can blame her for that? Her predecessor, Mary I, practically bankrupted England. England had an income of about £200,000 per year, but the high costs of defense and of European undercover activities far exceeded that. The only way she could raise the additional money was by selling lands owned by the Crown, by selling monopolies, and by asking Parliament to arrange for more taxes. Even then she had to resort to loans from foreign bankers. Her strong sense of fiscal responsibility meant that holding expenses to a minimum was de rigueur.

As we have said, England had problems with religious groups. The Catholics, not only in England but also in Spain and Rome, were always trying to get the country back into their fold. The Puritans were also bucking the Church of England and trying to increase their power and influence. It wasn't easy, but the queen managed to stay on top of things.

In this book, we are concerned primarily with the queen's relationship to the earl of Oxford. She had a special appreciation of his cultural and intellectual prowess. This was another of her great qualities, for she was open to the stimulating influence of the Renaissance. Although Elizabeth was seventeen years older, than the earl, there was an aura of sexual attraction. Could they have been lovers? I think so. After all, she was the daughter of Henry VIII. We don't blame a man for having an interest in younger women—why should we blame a woman for having an interest in a younger man, especially since she didn't have a husband? But the sexual point is secondary. The important thing here is that the earl *was* her favorite for a time. She loved to have him at her side, to dance, to present plays, to compose poetry. And after all, he was the third most important nobleman in England; only she and the duke of Norfolk preceded him. When Norfolk was beheaded for treason, Oxford assumed the second most important rank among the English nobility.

A word should be said about wards, since the earl of Oxford was a Queen's Ward. The tradition originated with feudalism. When a conquerer took over a country, he assumed control over all the land in his kingdom. A portion of this land was granted to three categories of people:

1. *oratores*—men who prayed;
2. *laboratores*—men who owed so many days of labor in the fields; and
3. *bellatores*—men who waged war.

The land given over in the first category was held by the Church until the Reformation, when it was repossessed, so to speak, by the king.

In the second category, the men involved were bound to the land: landed nobility who, in turn controlled men who tilled the soil. They could gain their freedom, but would have to sacrifice part of his property in order to do so.

After 1066, the Normans, and their successors handed out large tracts for military service to the bellatores. After all, the king needed helpers for defense purposes or to wage aggressive war. He also might have wanted to reward people who had helped him.

This system worked smoothly as long as the original receiver lived. But what would happen when he died? At that point, the children were beholden to fulfill the contract with the king, and thus he or she became a royal ward. The sovereign claimed control of the upbringing of the minor so as to obtain efficient service when the child came of age. In other words, he obtained wardship of the body. The mother had no rights, but she could buy out the wardship if she had the money. Usually she didn't, so, in effect, she lost her son.

If the ward was a female, the sovereign claimed the right to pick out her husband; otherwise, she might marry someone inimical to the sovereign. In this sense, the custom was a degradation of marriage. Forced marriages for purely mercenary reasons were common.

Over the years, some wardships disappeared. Records were lost; people died; new kings were created; When Henry VIII came along, however, he needed money badly, and one means to get income was to revive old wardships. In 1504, he used two flimsy legal means to reregister official records: "pour fille marier" (to marry off the daughter); and "pour faire fils chevalier" (to make a knight of the son).

The House of Commons resisted this move, giving him forty thousand pounds instead. In 1512, a new official title was created: the Master of Wards, to control concealed or forgotten wardships. In 1540, the Court of Wards was established to decide on the legal problems of wardships.

In the years 1535 to 1540, Henry VIII confiscated the monasteries and sold off their lands. In doing so, however, he established new wardships, which brought in annual rent and other fees. In a sense, he reestablished feudal dues—all this to provide for increasing national expenses.

If a tenant died while holding the land, then, his heir became a ward of the Crown. But his guardianship could be bought, and with it, his "marriage." If the wife picked out for him was not acceptable, the ward had to pay a crushing fine. Such was the case with the earl of Southampton: refusing to marry the young lady that Burghley had picked out to be his wife, he had to pay a fine of five thousand pounds.

Corruption and abuses crept in. All of this concerns Burghley, who is so important in understanding the Elizabethan era. Was he corrupt? Not in the ordinary sense, but, in accordance with existing practices, he got "gifts" for arranging things. Curiously, even though the number of fees and wardships increased under his management, the total income of the queen decreased.

The selling of wardships became big business. Let us see three examples from actual records:

A wardship that sold for £130 brought in an income of £38 per year;

One that sold for £14 brought in £4 yearly;

Another sold for £40 brought in £13 yearly.

The House of Commons wanted to put an end to the system of wardship. King James I, who succeeded Elizabeth, was willing to do so provided the Commons ensured financial security for the Crown. They couldn't get together on the financial details, however, so fiscal feudalism was kept alive. After all, money *was* needed. From Henry VII onward, all rulers ended their reigns in debt. The Commons eventually increased taxes to provide for expenses, forcing the Crown to give up royal prerogatives and setting the stage for today's relatively ceremonial sovereignty. In 1660, the Court of Wards was finally abolished.

The question of wardship played an important part in the lives of the earl of Oxford; Queen Elizabeth; Burghley and his son Robert; the earl of Southampton; and Anne (Oxford's wife).

A few more words should be said about Queen Mary of

Scotland, for she was fully involved in the life of Queen Elizabeth and almost as fully in the lives of the earl of Oxford and Lord Burghley. Mary really had a greater claim to the queenship of England than Elizabeth. Her claims went back to Henry VII, and in the eyes of Rome, her title was older and stronger. Moreover, Elizabeth, when she was born to Henry VIII and Anne Boleyn, was considered illegitimate by her own father.

Mary, born in 1542, was the daughter of James V of Scotland. As such, she inherited the title of Queen of Scotland while still a baby. At the age of sixteen, she was married to the Dauphin Francis of France, who became King Francis II in 1559. Her husband died a year later. Thus she held a double claim to the sovereignty.

Mary returned to Scotland to resume her reign. While many of the Scottish lords were Protestant, Mary was strongly Catholic. Even though Scotland was divided between Catholics and Protestants, however, both sides accepted Mary as queen.

There was a plot to marry Mary to the English duke of Norfolk, in which case she would have displaced Queen Elizabeth. The plot failed, however, and the duke of Norfolk was put to death, despite attempts by the earl of Oxford, who was related to the duke, to save him.

Shortly before that time, there was a rebellion of English Catholics in northern England, but English troops were sent out and quickly defeated the rebels. Queen Elizabeth, understandably fearful of future attempts, lashed out and had eight hundred of the rank and file hanged. The English crossed over into Scotland and made sure the rebels were taught a good lesson. The pillage and savaging destroyed three hundred villages and ninety fortified castles! It might be apropos to mention that Queen Elizabeth was not inactive in the move to foster Protestantism in Scotland. Indeed, she spent £200,000 in the pursuit of this movement. Mary, of course, wanted to make Scotland completely Catholic. The earl of Oxford was involved in some of this fighting. He must have received a great deal of material for his chronicle plays.

Queen Mary married her cousin, the English Lord Darnley. Misunderstandings arose when Darnley tried to assume more power than his wife was willing to give him. Eventually he was found murdered, and Mary's favorite, Bothwell, was strongly suspected of having engineered the act.

Bothwell soon divorced his wife and married Mary. This was too much for some of the Scottish lords. They forced her to abdicate in favor of her son, who was then declared James VI of Scotland. Bravely, she found herself heading a new army of six thousand men to help her resume power. The attempt failed and Mary fled to England, where she asked for the protection of her fellow sovereign, Queen Elizabeth. Mary was given asylum in England as a matter of protocol, even though she was a Catholic.

In that way, however, she became a lifetime prisoner of the English Queen. Continuing her intrigues to become queen of England, Mary was eventually convicted of treason and was executed in 1587.

Queen Elizabeth. (By permission of the National Portrait Gallery, London.)

5
The Looney Breakthrough

In previous chapters I have tried to show why Shaksper of Stratford could not possibly have written the plays and poetry of Shakespeare. I have cited examples in which unimportant writers or researchers have concocted the Stratford myth, simply because of the similarities of name. I have also reviewed the period's historical background, so that the reader may understand how certain things happened.

Soon after Shaksper's death, people began to doubt that the Stratford man could have written the plays. In 1785, Reverend James Wilmot of Warwickshire, in digging out facts, came to the assumption that Shaksper was illiterate. So were his parents and his daughters. Wilmot realized that the name "William Shakespeare" was a nom de plume. He decided that the true writer was Francis Bacon. For a time, this view was shared by many. The main trouble with this theory was that Bacon's style of writing was entirely different from that of Shakespeare.

In 1919, Professor Abel Le Franc of Belgium argued that the true Shakespeare was the earl of Derby. This theory also had holes in it, as did theories involving Queen Elizabeth herself; Mary Sidney, an outstanding poet and cultural leader; and Christopher Marlowe. There were many other candidates through the years, fifty-seven in all. All of them left much to be desired. A detective story was coming out, but without any real answers.

Why were there all these candidates? The simple reason is that it was difficult to think of the Stratford man as the real writer of the plays and sonnets.

At the end of World War I, an English schoolmaster, J. Thomas Looney (pronounced "Loney," as the "oo" in Roosevelt), who had been teaching Shakespeare's plays for many years, became convinced that the Stratford man could not have written the plays.

But then who did? Looney had no special candidate in mind but he did suspect that Oxford could have been the author, even though he knew very little about the man.

"Suppose," he reasoned, "we had found the plays without the name of the author. How would we go about trying to find his or her name?" Pursuing this idea, he made up a list of various characteristics evinced in the author's writings.

Looney concluded, after studying the works of Shakespeare, that the writer possessed the following special features:

1. recognized genius
2. eccentricity
3. unconventionality
4. pronounced literary tastes
5. enthusiasm for the drama
6. talent as a lyric poet
7. a superior education

In addition to these features, Looney stated, the true author of the Shakespeare's plays and poetry must have had the following characteristics:

1. feudal connections
2. membership in the higher aristocracy
3. connections with Lancastrian supporters
4. enthusiasm for Italy
5. an affiliation with sports, including falconry
6. a love of music
7. imprudence in money matters
8. a conflicted attitude toward women
9. a probable Catholic leaning

After he had made a profile of the mystery man, he reversed the process. Who were the known writers during the latter half of the sixteenth century? He checked off the characteristics against each author. In Bacon's case, for instance, the candidate had a classical education he knew law, and he was a Lancastrian. But he did not fit the other categories.

When it came to Edward de Vere, he checked out in *all* the

categories. The Stratford man checked out possibly in one: he might have had some interest in the theater.

Looney thus came to the conclusion that the name "Shakespeare" was a nom de plume for the earl of Oxford. In centering his research on Oxford, he found that everything meshed in beautifully. After his book, *Shakespeare Identified,* was published, the number of Oxfordian sympathizers, including other scholars, increased. The movement has been gaining strength ever since both in England and in the United States.

In 1937, Dr. Louis P. Benezet of Dartmouth College, a persistent Shakespeare scholar, made a tally of the Looney characteristics that appear in the main candidates for the authorship of the Shakespearean plays. His tally sheet is reproduced here.

But a check was done on another source, too: the *Dictionary of National Biography.* The article on the earl of Oxford bears out the following points that mesh with Looney's list of characteristics:

lyric poetry
eccentricity
genius
literary tastes
his liking for drama
aristocratic background
feudal ancestry
knowledge of Italy
looseness in money matters

The question arises: Why didn't other scholars see the earl of Oxford as the correct candidate? We must remember that there has been a deliberate plan to conceal all documentation related to the earl. It was probably the greatest conspiracy in history. Burghley, and undoubtedly Walsingham, with the reluctant acquiescence of the queen, had complete control of the mechanics of the plot. No one could dare to "blow the whistle," even if he knew what was taking place. Important manuscripts, documents, records, and correspondence have mysteriously disappeared from history. One good example: Burghley was careful to retain letters from his daughter pleading for her husband to return, but

	Classical education	Aristocrat	Warrior	Law student	Musician	Travel in Italy	Red Rose	Careless of money	A poet aside from "works"	Interested in theatre	Do the sonnets fit his life?	A playwright aside from "works"	Bore the canopy	Close association with Wriothesley
F. Bacon	yes	yes		yes										
E. de Vere	yes	yes	yes	yes	yes	yes	yes	yes	yes	yes	yes	yes	yes	yes
R. Manners	yes	yes	yes	yes	yes	yes		yes	yes	yes	yes		yes	yes
C. Marlowe	yes		yes					yes	yes	yes		yes		
W. Raleigh	yes	yes	yes	yes				yes	yes		yes			
W. Shakspere										yes?				
Mary Sidney	yes	yes			yes		yes	yes	yes	yes	yes			
W. Stanley	yes	yes	?	yes	yes		yes	yes	yes	yes		yes		

Source: *Shakspere, Shakespeare, and De Vere* (1937), by Louis P. Bénézet, A.M., Ph.D., professor at Dartmouth College.

curiously, kept not a single letter from Oxford to his wife. But then, it was also important to pass off a dummy person as the author. Because of the similarity in name, William Shaksper of Stratford was used. To a large degree, Burghley and his co-conspirators got away with it. Read the history books and the volumes on Shakespeare, and you will note that the earl of Oxford rarely surfaces.

Once Looney began to review the plays with the earl of Oxford in mind, he became certain that Oxford was the real Shakespeare. His important book, *Shakespeare Identified*, should be read by every lover of Shakespeare.

Unfortunately, as I have said, all university departments are wedded to the Stratford myth. The last thing most English professors would do is to encourage any of their students to read Looney. Because of this attitude, they are contributing to the greatest cover-up in literature. The people who control Stratford, and the professors in the English departments of our American colleges and universities are in effect perpetuating and abetting the work that Burghley started so efficiently.

Edward De Vere, Seventeenth Earl of Oxford. From a portrait by Marcus Gheeraedts.

6
Who Was the Earl of Oxford?

We have mentioned Edward de Vere, the seventeenth earl of Oxford, in preceding chapters. After Looney pointed out the earl as the most feasible candidate for the authorship of the Shakespearean plays and poems, then many, if not most of the Shakespearean scholars who had discounted Shaksper of Stratford as the author began to concentrate their attention on the earl. The fountainhead of this research was Looney. As people began trying to solve the puzzle, it became increasingly evident that the earl of Oxford must have been the real Shakespeare. Despite his absence in existing books on Shakespeare, everything seemed to fit.

Edward de Vere was born on 22 April 1550, at Castle Hedingham, to an outstanding family whose roots went back to William the Conqueror. The family had come from the village of Ver in Normandy, France. For more than five hundred years, members of this family had served England. One member had married the sister of William the Conqueror. Another had been among the nobles who had forced King John to sign the Magna Carta. Still another had contributed to the famous victory of Henry V at Agincourt. In the War of the Roses, the de Veres fought on the Lancastrian side to overthrow Richard III at Bosworth Field. No one in England, not even Queen Elizabeth, could boast of a greater pedigree. After the execution of the duke of Norfolk, Oxford was, after the queen, the most prestigious noble in the country. In a sense, Burghley was a parvenu on the scene.

The seventeenth earl of Oxford, our Shakespeare, was understandably proud of his family's history. He also found himself living in a period when feudalism was coming to an end and the commercial classes gaining prominence, signaling the development of the English nation as we know it today. One can understand the feelings that might have developed between the nobleman Edward de Vere and his father-in-law, Lord Burghley, who was a prime example of the aspiring middle class.

De Vere received the best education possible in England during the sixteenth century. In 1559, he matriculated at St. John's College, Cambridge. When he was twelve years of age, his father died. At this point, reread the paragraph I wrote on the subject of wards. The young earl, now the seventeenth in his line, became the Queen's Ward. She assigned him to William Cecil (later Lord Burghley), who became his guardian.

Cecil founded an outstanding school for royal wards in England, acquiring the best books available and establishing an excellent library. The young earl had the best tutors that anyone could have in England. One was Sir Thomas Smith, Regius Professor of Civil Law, who eventually became the principal secretary of state. Another tutor was Lawrence Nowell, later dean of Litchfield. From John Gerarde, probably the best herbalist in England, the young earl learned about flowers and plants. The famed astronomer, Dr. John Dee, undoubtedly taught him all there was to know about the stars and the heavens.

Oxford was an outstanding student: a voracious reader, a careful observer, an avid learner. It is easy to understand how he absorbed the background of knowledge that is evident in his plays. Compare this with the apparent lack of schooling in the case of the Stratford Shaksper before, during, or after his relatively brief stay in London.

Oxford's education was entrusted to his uncle, Arthur Golding, an outstanding scholar of the classics. In the meantime, Oxford's mother seems to have married, with "unseeming haste," a Charles Tyrrell. As a ward, the young earl was, therefore, brought up in the household of William Cecil. In 1564, he received a degree from Cambridge, and a year later he was awarded the master of arts degree from Oxford.

In 1567, his uncle's translation of Ovid's Latin work, *Metamorphoses,* was published. The young student must have been imbued with the love of this classic, and some scholars feel that he may have actually done some or all of the English versification.

In 1567, Oxford began his legal studies. He was admitted to Gray's Inn in London, a school and professional training institution for students of the law. It was here that he acquired the law background evident in his plays.

At this point, the young earl was involved in a tragedy in the Cecil household. He wounded with his sword a servant who was hiding behind a tapestry, apparently spying on him. The victim died, but Oxford was exonerated. Whether his guardian, William Cecil, ordered the man to spy is not known, but, at any rate, the scene is recreated in *Hamlet*.

In 1570, Oxford enlisted under the earl of Sussex in the campaign in Scotland, when the queen was waging war against Catholic rebels. While there, he undoubtedly observed events and details that appeared later in his chronicle plays.

In 1571, Queen Elizabeth probably arranged for Oxford to marry Anne Cecil, the fourteen-year-old daughter of his guardian. In wardships, you will remember, this was a perfectly normal procedure. In this case, however, there was a hitch: a noble could not marry a commoner, which Anne was. To solve the problem, the queen ennobled William Cecil, making him Lord Burghley. There was no objection, of course, from William Cecil, who had planned to marry his daughter to Philip Sidney. As with most of the royal marriages in those days, it wasn't based on love, but Anne was probably dazzled by being married to such an important noble. Oxford at first resisted the match, but according to the accepted rules of procedure, he finally had to acquiesce.

Just as the wedding arrangements were being made, an important event occurred. The duke of Norfolk, England's foremost nobleman, became involved in a plot to put Mary, Queen of Scotland, on the throne of England, with himself as her husband. As a result, he was charged with treason. Oxford, related to Norfolk, undoubtedly pleaded with the queen to save the duke's life. The queen agonized over this for more than a year but finally decided not to stay the execution.

Oxford, now twenty-one, had become a favorite at the court, participating with vigor and outstanding success in the jousts held there. We have here the first image of Oxford as a "spear-shaker," a term that could have suggested the nom de plume, "Shake-speare."

Incidentally, if Lord Burghley was a harsh and meddling father-in-law, Oxford's mother-in-law was even worse. Stern and vigilant, she deeply resented the monopoly that the queen held on her son-in-law's time, which took him into the life of the Court and away from his wife. She did not hesitate to rebuke the queen for doing so.

Of course, this unhappy state of affairs was caused by the feudalistic practice of wardship, whereby the queen had the right to control the marriage of her royal ward. In the meantime, Lord Burghley, as guardian of the royal ward, profited greatly from Oxford's marriage to his daughter. Alas, forced marriages do not produce happy marriages, and so it was with Oxford and his childlike wife, Anne Cecil.

It should be stated that Oxford had a rival in his standing as a court favorite—Christopher Hatton. Later, in discussing the volume *A Hundreth Sundrie Flowres*, we shall come upon a striking literary duel with Hatton.

During 1572, Oxford openly gave evidence of his wish to be a writer. His former tutor at Cambridge, Bartholomew Clerke, had translated the famous book of Baldassare Castiglione, *Il Cortegiano*, from Italian into Latin. This book, emanating from the Renaissance court of the duke of Urbino in Italy, presented the image of the ideal courtier. Oxford, in a lengthy preface in Latin, clearly announced to the world that he was interested in important books and that he liked to write. Moreover, he added his name and title to the title page and evidently also bore the expense for the publication of the book.

It was now 1573. As has been stated, the marriage with Anne Cecil was not a happy one. Oxford did not live with his wife, preferring to spend his time in the company of other writers. He naturally paid all the expenses of this arrangement. His behavior provoked the utter displeasure of his father-in-law, Lord Burghley.

An important development took place during this year. A Thomas Bedingfield did a Latin translation of a book titled *Comforte*, by an Italian author, Girolamo Cardano. Oxford wrote a preface, which gave him an opportunity to do some more lengthy writing. Again, he was probably subsidizing the publication. So now we have Oxford involved with two books, *Il Cortegiano* by Castiglione, and Cardano's *Comforte*. There is no question about Oxford's ability to write or about his interest in literature. But more important, ideas expressed in both books crop up in his plays. In *Hamlet*, for instance, the prince of Denmark is the perfect example of the ideal courtier. Furthermore, philosophic ideas expressed in *Comforte* can be seen in the soliloquy, "To be or not to be."

Also in 1573, Henry Wriothesly (pronounced Rosely) was born. He was to become the third earl of Southampton. Was he the illegitimate son of the earl of Oxford? Although it has never been proven, I believe he was.

It must be pointed out that no Englishman could leave the country without permission from the queen, just as people from the Soviet Union and other dictatorships today need permission from the state to leave their countries.

In 1574, Oxford escaped to the continent without permission. Undoubtedly, he was restless—perhaps angry that he was no longer the court favorite, perhaps anxious to get away from his wife and in-laws. The queen, perturbed at his action, sent his former tutor, Thomas Bedingfield, to urge him to return. Oxford did so reluctantly, evidently finding his way back into the good graces of the queen.

The next year, he did receive reluctant permission to travel to the continent. His father-in-law tried to discourage the trip, probably because he didn't want his son-in-law to leave his wife and because such a trip was very costly. He would have to travel with a retinue of eight people, and in fact, Oxford had to sell a number of his estates to pay for the trip.

In March and April of 1575, Oxford visited the court of Catherine de Medici in France, and was received by King Henry II. The royal court was then at Blois. He went on to visit the German scholar, Johannes Sturmius, in Strasbourg. For the next ten or eleven months, he traveled in Italy. This part of his trip had such an important influence on his life and works that I am treating it in a separate chapter. In mid-September, Oxford learned that his wife had given birth to a daughter, Elizabeth.

In March of 1576, he returned to Paris, where it was whispered to him that the daughter, Elizabeth, was not really his. He rushed back to England, greatly angered that he had been cuckolded, and refused to speak to his wife or to Lord Burghley. For the next five years, he remained estranged from his wife. This experience is reflected in several of his plays, but especially in *Othello* and *Measure for Measure*.

As I go along, I occasionally give examples of parallel allusions in the plays to the life of Oxford. These are but samples, for otherwise this chapter would become a heavy tome in itself. But those interested in pursuing this parallelism can turn to one of four books:

The Mysterious William Shakespeare, by
    Charlton Ogburn, Jr.;

Shakespeare Identified, by
    J. Thomas Looney (edited in two volumes by Ruth Lloyd Miller);

This Star of England, by
    Dorothy and Charlton Ogburn, Sr.; and

Hidden Allusions in Shakespeare's Plays, by
    Eva Turner Clark.

A piece of evidence dating from 1578 establishes the earl of Oxford as a poet. Gabriel Harvey, a fellow at Trinity College, Cambridge, in an address to the queen at an important university occasion, hailed Oxford as a prolific poet, and one whose "countenance shakes spears."

The following year, there was performed at court a play, *The Historie of the Second Helene,* which was an early version of *All's Well That Ends Well.* Another play performed at court, *A Morrall of the Marryage of Mynde and Measure,* was an early version of *The Taming of the Shrew.* (Note also that all this was too early to fit in with the Shaksper dates). Still another play, the History of *Portio and Demorantes,* performed in 1580 likely led to the later *Merchant of Venice* and *Twelfth Night.* None of the plays had Oxford's name as author. Nobles just didn't append their names to plays.

At this point let me briefly explain a point that may otherwise cause confusion: The earl of Oxford held the title of "Lord *Great* Chamberlain." This was a hereditary title, a ceremonial one used only at certain state occasions. Oxford refers to these occasions in sonnet 125: "Weren't aught to me I bore the canopy." As lord great chamberlain, you see, he had the hereditary honor of helping to hold the canopy over the queen's head.

The lord chamberlain, on the other hand, was an entirely different position, involved in making arrangements, under royal patronage, for the presentation of plays at the court, and also for the licensing of plays and theaters for the public. A company of actors under the patronage of lord chamberlain presented many of Shakespeare's plays.

In 1580 Oxford, who, as we know, had Catholic leanings, was drawn unwittingly into an incipient Catholic plot to do away with the Protestant Queen Elizabeth. When he realized the danger to the queen and to England, he revealed everything to the queen, accusing Henry Howard, the earl of Arundel, and Francis Southwell. I have already mentioned that Arundel, to buy time, in turn accused Oxford of many heinous offenses. The queen didn't know whom to believe, but was put on her guard. Eventually, Oxford's accusation turned out to be true.

Let us consider at this point the historic preferences of the earl of Oxford. He was a Lancastrian, as opposed to belonging to the House of York. English history is full of periods in which one branch of a royal family tries to take over the power of another. Those of Lancastrian sympathy adopted the red rose as their symbol; the Yorkists a white rose—hence the name, the Wars of the Roses. A knowledge of this phase of English history will be useful in understanding the chronicle plays and also Oxford's bias toward the Lancastrian side.

In 1580, because of expenses incurred by his subsidy of literary activities, style of living, and trip to Europe, Oxford had to sell off thirteen of his estates.

The year 1581 turned out to be a crucial year in Oxford's life. He had an affair with Anne Vavasor, a lady at court. A baby was born; both Oxford and Anne were sent to the Tower. Queen Elizabeth didn't want her courtiers and ladies involved in court scandals. Now, it must not be assumed that the Tower was entirely a dank, foul prison. Part of it was a sort of genteel, comfortable house of detention. I suppose Oxford and Anne Vavsor were both assigned suites. Food was brought in, and guests could visit.

Incidentally, Charles Barrell, the researcher, whom I have mentioned, uncovered most of the facts regarding Anne Vavasor. She is Rosaline in *Love's Labour's Lost;* she is also the "dark lady" in the *Sonnets* of Shakespeare. We know, therefore, that Oxford had a son by Anne and that his name was Edward Vere. He always watched over his son, making sure that he was given a proper education and military opportunities.

The Vavasor affair was to have ugly consequences, however. Anne's uncle, Thomas Knyvet, swore revenge. As a result, there was a continuing feud between his followers and those of Oxford, somewhat like that between the Montagues and the Capulets in *Romeo and Juliet.* In one altercation, Oxford was probably cut in the leg by a sword, becoming lamed for life. He referred to his lameness a number of times in his verses. In Sonnets 89 and 37, he wrote: "Speak of my lameness and I straight will halt." Later he says, "So I, made lame by fortune's dearest spite."

Incidentally, Anne Vavasor must have been quite a two-timing lady. She had a succession of love affairs. She eventually married a John Finche, but later left him to live in adultery with a Sir Henry Lee.

Lord Oxford steadfastly loved Edward, his illegitimate son by Anne Vavasor. He bemoaned the fact that the boy, then eight years of age, should have to grow up within a household of adultery. While Oxford could not openly acknowledge the boy as his son, he watched over him tenderly. When the lad reached the age of fourteen, he was sent away for a better rearing. He received military training under the supervision of his cousins, Horatio and Francis Vere, and was sent to Europe, where he attended the University of Leyden. The youth kept up his studies in literature and in history. In 1607, Edward Vere was knighted by King James I, and in 1623, he became a member of Parliament.

While Oxford was engaged in the many literary activities that we have noted, what was our Stratford man, William Shaksper, doing? Well, in 1582, he was forced to marry Anne Hathaway because she was pregnant. So far, there isn't a word mentioned by anybody that he had any literary proclivities.

In 1583, Oxford acquired a sublease on the Blackfriars Theatre in London, but it had to be transferred to John Lyly, who was a sort of manager for him. The role of the theatre is somewhat muddled, and the records are not very clear. Some of this uncertainty and confusion was probably caused by Burghley in his plan to sanitize the records of his son-in-law. What is clear, however, is that Oxford was running low on funds. He was down to four servants, which was indeed stinting for an outstanding nobleman. But this is important: at court, there was presented under his patronage *Agamemnon and Ulysses* the first version of *Troilus and Cressida.*

By this time, Oxford had his own company of actors, who toured the provinces when they were not playing in London. During 1583 and 1584, this company performed at Stratford. It could be that the Stratford Shaksper either was invited to join this company as a servitur, or of his own volition became a hanger-on.

Looking boldly at the record, there is no evidence of an exciting marriage on the part of Shaksper, who had no compunction in leaving his wife and two young daughters. When he died, he left her the "second-best bed."

We have noted that under another name, Oxford's company presented an early version of *Troilus and Cressida* at court. The record of his presentation of plays at the court should alone be enough to establish the legitimacy of Oxford's authorship. As in the preparation of all plays, these evolved from primary versions to corrections and finally to finished works.

In 1585, in an attempt to straighten out his finances, Oxford unwisely invested in the outfitting of a ship to find a northwest passage to Asia through what is now Canada. This was a common form of capitalistic venture in the sixteenth century. The risks were great, but if a project turned out well, the returns could be fabulous. In this case, Oxford lost everything he gambled. Only an Oxfordian, therefore can understand the seemingly meaningless phrase in *Hamlet,* "mad north by northwest."

The plays also offer evidence of Oxford's extensive legal knowledge. At the 1584 session of the House of Commons, Oxford was named one of the Triers of Petitions. Serving on the same committee were Raleigh and Oxford, who were interested in explorations for new colonies in America. The committee was charged with looking into the matter.

Oxford's legal knowledge proved of great help to him as a member of Parliament. In 1588, he became a ranking member of a second committee, retaining that position until his death in 1604. In his plays, he frequently uses legal concepts. For example, the word "petition" is found twenty-five times; the word "trier," a synonym for "auditor," is found three times. Thus, Oxford's understanding of the law is amply reflected by both his position in Parliament and by his plays.

To return to the subject of Oxford's financial situation: We learn that in 1586, the queen assigned him one thousand pounds per year. No accounting for this grant was to be made. The grant was not to be continued to his heirs. To this day, no one knows why such a large grant was made, for it was larger than anything on record and for no specific service. Some believe it as for the writing of patriotic plays. Others say it was to support Oxford's dramatic activities.

Just about this time, Southampton is said to have paid one thousand pounds to the Stratford Shaksper. Could it be that some of the payment by the queen was being "laundered" through Southampton to Shaksper? There is no evidence that Oxford's standard of living was ameliorated in any way. Besides, Queen Elizabeth was noted for her stinginess. Why should she make such an exaggerated grant to anyone? She just didn't throw money around that way.

On the other hand, all of a sudden, the Stratford man apparently received a great deal of money, £250 quarterly, or £1000 per year, according to one person. And in Lady de Vere's will, there was a provision for payment to "my dombe man," who probably was Shaksper. How else could the Stratford man account for such sudden riches? Plays brought in very little, acting even less. No, I think that (1) Shaksper of Stratford was given the immense sum to lend out his name in the plot to ascribe the authorship of the Oxford's plays to someone else; and (2) the set-up was concocted by Burghley in order to prevent recognition of characters and events in the plays.

Another piece of evidence that Oxford was known as a poet dates from the same year, 1586. William Webbe, in his volume *A Discourse of English Poetry*, speaks of the earl of Oxford as "most excellent among the rest."

One way of solving the puzzle of whether the earl of Oxford was Shakespeare is to compare the characteristics of a poem written by Oxford in his youth with those of Shakespeare's poetry. Such a comparison was one means Looney used to identify the true Shakespeare. Looney observed that Oxford used the six-line stanza, *ababcc*, with each line having ten syllables.

In another example, one of Oxford's early poems refers to "haggards," a term used in falconry. Haggards are imperfectly trained hawks that fly from man to man. Oxford compares them to inconstant women who go from one man to another:

> Like haggards wild they range,
> These gentle birds that fly from man to man.
> Who would not scorn and shake them from the fist
> And let them fly, fair fools, which way they list?

The same idea is used in *Othello:*

> If I do find her haggard,
> Though that her jesses were my heart strings,
> I'd whistle her off, and let her down the wind
> To play at fortune.
>
> 3.3.264–67

A jess, incidentally, is a short strap fastened to the leg of a hawk.

The term also appears in *The Taming of the Shrew* (4.1), and in *Much Ado About Nothing* (3.1).

Looney found many other parallelisms. For instance, one line of Oxford's poetry is:

> And let her moan and none lament her need.

In his poem *The Rape of Lucrece*, written under the name "Shakespeare," there occurs a line:

> To make him moan, but pity not his moans.

Here is still another example from an Oxford poem:

> O cruel hap and hard estate,
> That forceth me to love my foe.

Shakespeare writes in *Romeo and Juliet:*

> Prodigious birth of love it is to me,
> That I must love a loathed enemy.

There is yet a further piece of evidence. As a premier earl, Oxford had to participate in the trial of Mary, Queen of Scots. Her plea for mercy is mirrored in Portia's speech in *The Merchant of Venice*.

The year 1588 is, of course, the date when the English defeated the Spanish Armada. It was a watershed happening for a small nation. From then on, the Spanish empire began to decline; by contrast, the English nation acquired the confidence of victory.

Let us return once again to the subject of feudalistic practices. While on one hand, the queen was beginning to build a navy, it was still the practice of the nobles to pitch in with their own help. In this case, Oxford, even though he was "broke," contributed the ship "Edward Bonaventure" to the fray. It didn't have too great a role.

It was during this year, 1588, that Oxford's wife, Anne, died. Burghley, who had been watching over his daughter, took over the granddaughter, as was permitted under the wardship system. He also took over the finances of his former ward, the earl of Oxford. The following year, he sued for the marriage fee that had never been paid.

Burghley tried to marry off his granddaughter, Elizabeth, to the earl of Southampton, not knowing that he was her half-brother (if our assumption is correct). Southampton would have none of it. Now, Southampton, like Oxford, was also a Queen's Ward under the guardianship of Burghley. For refusing to accept the marriage, and according to wardship rules as I have explained them, Southampton had to pay a whopping fee of five thousand pounds. Can you understand why the House of Commons in 1660 put an end to this archaic system?

Also during the year 1588, Oxford reworked *As You Like It* into its present form. I must point out, however, that all of Shakespeare's plays were in a state of constant flux. We do not know whether any of the plays as we have them today are the finished edition as Oxford considered them. Even after 1623, there were changes made in future folios.

Meanwhile, Oxford's finances were worsening. He had to disband his acting company. He also had to sell two other properties that were dear to him, Fisher's Folly, which was a gathering place for his fellow writers, and the Vere house.

In 1591, probably because he needed financial resuscitation, he married Elizabeth Trentham, a wealthy widow of noble bearing. Under the rules of wardship, Oxford had to have the permission of the queen, which she gave willingly. So began a peaceful period in Oxford's life, unspoiled by financial problems and the responsibilities of theater productions. He was free to consider his plays not in terms of their immediate production but as works of literature to be read. The hassles with his former father-in-law ended. The new marriage seems to have been a happy and serene one. His wife gave him freedom from financial worries. She also gave him the tender, loving care and quiet he needed to revise his plays. These were probably in a disorderly state, as they had been dashed off for stage use and corrected as the occasion demanded. In the meantime, nothing is known of the Stratford Shaksper.

The exact date at which the name "William Shakespeare" and later, "William Shake-speare" was appended by publishers to the various works is not known exactly. Scholars assign various dates, in some cases to suit the requirements of the Stratford myth. We do know that in 1598, *Love's Labour's Lost* and *Henry Fourth, Part I* were published under the name W. Shakespeare. Why did Oxford suddenly decide to write with a pen name? We can only speculate. What could be the different reasons? Possibly he had to protect himself against the pirating of his plays. I don't think so. Or perhaps the first phase of the Stratford plot was in the making—an order was given from higher up to find a pseudonym. At any rate, it made sense to have a pseudonym, and the "shaker" of "spears" easily adopted "Shakespeare."

In 1593, *Venus and Adonis,* a poem, was entered at the Stationers' Register. It was dedicated to the earl of Southampton and signed "William Shakespeare." In 1594, *The Rape of Lucrece* surfaced—registered and signed. Still nothing is known of our friend Shaksper, although Stratfordians concoct all sorts of activities out of thin air. In 1595, Oxford's daughter, Elizabeth, married the sixth earl of Derby. This was one of the couples who probably helped to pay for the First Folio in 1623.

In the meantime, Shakespearean plays were being published and produced.

In 1598, another piece of evidence appeared: Francis Meres, in his *Palladis Tamia*, mentioned *Shakespeare* among those "best for comedy." Meres was used by those dictating the plot to show that Oxford and Shakespeare were two different persons. Oxfordians use Meres to prove he did write comedies. Stratfordians, sweeping this statement under the rug, speak only of the tragedies.

In 1603, Queen Elizabeth died. She was succeeded by James I (he had been James VI of Scotland), the son of Queen Mary of Scotland, who all her life had plotted to supplant Elizabeth. The next year, the earl of Oxford died. As a mark of respect, James I had seven of Shakespeare's plays presented at court. Is this not another link in the Oxfordian stance? Oxford's wife died in 1612 and, as I have stated, in her will made provisions for a certain number of pounds to be paid "to my dombe man." Was this a continuance of money to be paid to Shaksper to keep his mouth shut?

In 1622, a Henry Peacham listed *Edward de Vere*, not Shakespeare, as one of the poets who made the Elizabethan era a golden age.

In 1623, the First Folio was published. It was dedicated to the earl of Pembroke and the earl of Montgomery. The title: *Mr. William Shakespeare's Comedies, Histories, & Tragedies*. Thirty-six plays were included, eighteen of which had never before been published. The two to whom the volume is dedicated must have been the ones to defray the heavy cost of publication. The First Folio included four poems lauding Shakespeare, Ben Jonson's being the longest.

Looney has divided the life of Shakespeare (i.e., Oxford) into three periods:

The Early Period extends from birth (1550) to his return from the European trip in 1576.

The Middle Period extends from 1576, when he sets up his artistic atelier, so to speak, until 1588, when his wife Anne dies. During this period he worked actively with the theater group he had brought together and was supporting. The group played in London, but also toured the provinces.

The Final Period covers the years from 1590 to Oxford's death in 1604. He seems to have quit the responsibilities of the theater, having reached the nadir of his financial position. Having married a lady of wealth, however, he was able to spend the rest of his life changing his theater pieces into literature.

Regarding Oxford's handwriting, we have examples of his letters written in beautiful script, as is evidenced in the letter we have reproduced on page 102. Apparently, the finished or almost-finished drafts of his plays were not available to the Grand Possessors, those putting the project together. It would almost seem that this was one aspect of the plot. Oxford's calligraphy would be easily identified. Therefore, the strategy may have been to collect any copies written by him and either hide them or destroy them.

If, in fact, the copies written by Oxford were hidden, let us hope that one of these days these manuscripts will be found. What a revolutionary happening that would be!

Mr. WILLIAM
SHAKESPEARES
COMEDIES,
HISTORIES, &
TRAGEDIES.

Published according to the True Originall Copies.

LONDON
Printed by Isaac Iaggard, and Ed. Blount. 1623.

Title Page of 1623 First Folio. Note the trumped-up drawing by Droeshout.

7
Publishing and the Theater

It is germane to our discussion to know a little about the publishing practices of Elizabethan times. First of all, some books, tracts, or poems circulated in manuscript form from person to person. There was, at the same time, a certain amount of trade carried on in handwritten copies of books. Other books could be printed, provided they had been approved by the censors.

An important event in the book trade took place in 1557, with the incorporation of the Stationers' Company, which included both publishers and booksellers. It constituted the official authority over England's entire book trade. With the approval of its charter by Queen Elizabeth in 1559, the company began to exercise its power of censorship throughout her reign. Under its charter, no person could print any book, pamphlet, play, or poem without its or the queen's permission. The archbishop of Canterbury and York; the bishop of London; and the chancellors of Cambridge and Oxford acted for the Stationers' Company.

In 1586, a limit on the number of printing presses was decreed in London, Cambridge, and Oxford. Severe punishments were established for those operating any secret presses. Let us remember that the Catholic Church in Rome had secretly landed a number of Jesuits in England, whose purpose it was to strengthen the role of the Catholics and to establish a secret press for the printing of its tracts. The Puritans, at least until they came into power, were also known to print secret tracts in order to bring in converts and multiply their number. Opposed to the Church of England, they wanted to establish their own form of Protestantism.

Then the Stationers' Company established a register, which was really an early form of the copyright arrangement. Such a register would give us a record of any publications bearing on Shakespeare. The earl of Oxford would write out the parts for the plays he composed, giving them directly to the actors. Each actor received his own part, marked with cues to indicate where he came in. Surreptitiously, printers would make up the plays recited by the actors. Since the plays had not been registered, they could do so with impunity. The Stratford Shaksper, being a commoner, could involve himself with the theatre without fear of repercussions. The fee to register was nominal. Since we know he was inclined to protect his rights strongly, he certainly would have protected the right to his plays. Having paid the fee, he would have had the sole rights to printing or publishing for the future.

It might be interesting to note that in 1586, the Stationers' Company ordered that no more than 1,250 copies of a book should be printed. After that, the type had to be taken apart. This was an early form of union featherbedding, intended to enable the compositors to get a "fair" part of the business. Incidentally, 500 to 600 copies were probably printed of the First Folio.

There you have the general picture of the publishing business during the Elizabethan era. Undoubtedly, there were trespasses of the law, and, if the case were not too serious, some tolerance of minor lapses. But the whole situation was small and limited enough that the authorities could easily find out what was going on. Censorship flourished, a situation not unlike that in the Soviet Union today. The control was of a religious, political, and moral character, but especially political, which in turn boiled down to theological purposes. Curiously, the Puritans, who came into control after the Elizabethan era, developed into the most severe censors of all.

We know that at certain periods the earl of Oxford was close to the queen. As a noble, he could not append his name to poems or plays. In his careless youth, he had written a few poems and added his initials. For this he was duly chastised by being banned from the court. For some time afterward, he had to write his plays anonymously. The printers had a merry time cashing in on those plays, which were floating around unregistered and uncopyrighted. Then came the period in which Oxford was forced to write under a pseudonym.

Did Shaksper deal in Shakespeare plays? Did some people confused William Shaksper with William Shakespeare? Did

Shaksper encourage the deception? All are possibilities. Did Burghley arrange the deception? That is certain.

I told you it was a great detective story.

Now, a few words should be said about the theater in London because Oxford is involved directly. What are the salient points?

We know that groups of players would present their offerings in the courtyards of inns and taverns, or wherever the plays could get a crowd to listen to them. They could rely on money offerings from the public.

We know that Queen Elizabeth was keenly interested in holding dramatic and poetry presentations at court. She also encouraged her noblemen to arrange such offerings. Those few noblemen who could afford to maintain a company of players would have the presentations during the Christmas season, or perhaps when the queen was visiting them on her various tours throughout the land. To gain extra income, the troupe of subsidized players would go on tour throughout England.

Another point about the theater is that the lord chamberlain was in general charge of both court presentations and any plays offered to the public. The Office of the Revels had been established under his jurisdiction in 1550. This office, a department of the royal household, was in direct charge of setting up plays and masques at the court. A masque, incidentally, was a nondramatic performance involving masks, colorful costumes, lighted torches, dancing, music, drums, and general revelry. Later, a certain dramatic element was introduced. "Revels" meant simply theatrical entertainment at court. The hall at the court measured about forty feet wide and about one hundred feet long. The cost of such royal programs was about five hundred pounds, a hefty sum. This may be one reason the queen encouraged her nobles to present shows to her on her travels: to get some free entertainment.

The sixteenth earl of Oxford was among the small group of nobles who maintained a player's group. Their presentations gave the young Edward de Vere his first exposure to the theatre.

B. M. Ward, in his outstanding biographical work, *The Seventeenth Earl of Oxford*, states that in 1586, a Richard Farrant and a William Hunnis "first conceived the idea of a theatre open to the public on payment, where the Choir Boys could also be rehearsed before appearing at Court." This theater was a room at the Blackfriars Convent. In the book *Shakespeare's England*, William Archer and W. J. Lawrence refer to this theater as a "private theater." I believe that it was "private" because of the law that forbade public theaters in the city proper. The date given by them is 1576. Farrant died shortly thereafter, but Hunnis continued in the theater until 1583, when he sold the lease to a Henry Evans. The latter transferred it to Oxford, who then assigned his secretary, John Lyly, to manage it. Note that Oxford, as a nobleman with entrée to the court, and as a favorite of the queen, was in an excellent position to effect what was really the birth of the public theater in England.

The first real theater built in England was that of James Burbage in 1576, simply called "The Theater," a shortened form of "amphitheatre." It was a decided improvement over the helter-skelter performances in taverns, inns, and other locations. Plays could also be rehearsed before being presented at court. Even Oxford probably rehearsed some of his plays here before having them presented at court. Oxford undoubtedly composed early plays to be presented at court. Shakespearean scholar Eva Turner Clark notes that, according to the court calendar, the following plays were performed. These plays fell under the direction of the lord chamberlain of the household, the earl of Sussex, who was through the years a warm friend of Oxford:

1. 1578: *An history of the cruelties of A Stepmother*
2. 1579: *The historie of the second Helene*
3. 1579: *A Maske of Amazones and a Maske of Knights*
4. 1579: *The history of murderous Michael*

These four plays, as well as eight additional ones, all surface later with different titles, under the name of Shakespeare: *Cymbeline; All's Well That Ends Well; Love's Labour's Lost;* and *Arden of Feversham.*

It would help us to understand the Shakespeare question if we knew how plays were produced in the sixteenth century. The writer or the producer did not give out complete copies of the play to the actors. As I mentioned earlier, each actor got his own part; these were collected when he had memorized the lines. This was to prevent pirating of the plays. Now, of course, it might be possible for a pirate publisher to get the individual actors to recite their parts; he might thereby refashion the plays, even filling in with fake lines if necessary.

We should mention the attitude of the Puritans toward the theater. They felt it was the work of the devil. Since 1576 they had fought against it. Had it not been for the encouragement that Queen Elizabeth gave to the theater in general, they would have succeeded in doing away with public presentations. This didn't occur until 1642, when the Puritans shut down all the theaters during the Civil War.

All of this directly affects our Oxford story. In 1580, the year Oxford started a company of actors, he sold thirteen of his estates. There is no evidence that he was living in a luxurious style. In fact, we have the statement of his father-in-law, Burghley, that Oxford was down to four servants, strict economy for a noble. In 1583, according to Shakespearean researcher B. M. Ward, there was a queen's company of actors composed of twelve men (a measure of her determination to strengthen the English theater). There undoubtedly was collaboration between her efforts and those of Oxford. And, Lord Oxford's "company of choir boys," a group separate from his adult group, must have cooperated with the queen's group to supply the female characters (boys were used for female roles at that time). The records show that Lyly, who was manager of Oxford's company, also presented plays for the queen's group.

We have seen, therefore, that the theater had two developments. One was thoroughly plebeian, characterized by troupes who eked out a living by presenting plays or other entertainment wherever they could draw a crowd. At the opposite pole was the royal presentation. Somewhere in between were the groups of young apprentices, boys who were taking the parts of women's characters and were thus acquiring the training for court presentations. The earl of Oxford was the leading figure in bringing these developments together, for two reasons: he was an outstanding noble, and he was willing to spend the money and work both at court and in the public theater. To be sure, he was criticized by Burghley for consorting with "lewd" people. Furthermore, he was from 1570 to 1580, a distinct favorite of the queen who, like him, was an enthusiast of play productions. In a sense, then, Oxford was a catalytic agent in the development of the theater in England. His trip to Italy in 1575–76 was a great spur to his imagination. He had seen some theater in France, but in Italy he saw a number of theatrical productions, and this gave him an opportunity to observe the mechanics of the stage and the development of characters. While he had already read many Italian sources, here he had an opportunity to buy more books and to gain new sources of material.

To recapitulate what we have said elsewhere, Oxford's life can be divided into three periods. The first is a period of preparation. The second begins after he returns from Italy. He plunges into his playwriting activities and starts his own theater, which Lyly manages. He is also involved with court presentations. It is a period full of the rough-and-tumble aspects of play-producing and the pressures of pleasing the public. In 1589, he retires from theatrical production and turns his attention to the adaption of his own plays for literature.

The Grand Possessors apparently could not put their hands on the original and finished copies of the plays. I believe that these finished copies in the neat and easily recognized calligraphy of the earl of Oxford are missing because they would constitute an easy proof of his authorship. Burghley must have had them either destroyed or hidden somewhere. Let us hope that it is the latter, and that someday they will come to light.

An afterthought should be included here. Shakespeare supposedly owned a share in the rebuilt Blackfriars Theatre. If Shakespeare were the Stratford man, why did Shakesper not include the ownership in his will? Could it have been part of the ploy to give the Stratford man the coloration of the real writer? The record is unclear.

Also unclear is the difference between a "private" theater and a "public" theater. Because of the higher admission charge, the private theater was perhaps a more genteel place. It had artificial lighting, a smaller setting, and seating for everyone.

There was an inconsistency in the public and the courtly attitude toward the theater. Despite the public's support and the queen's encouragement of the theater, there was a social stigma on the actor. To top it all, the Puritans wanted to do away with the theater altogether. It is amazing that the institution survived, and in fact it was banned during the Cromwellian period.

8
The Plot

The plot to disguise Shakespeare's true identity was probably hatched by Oxford's father-in-law, Lord Burghley. There was no love lost between the two men. To be sure, there were times when Burghley had to get along with his son-in-law. After all, if he hurt Oxford, his daughter would suffer as well. But when his daughter died, he no longer had any need to help Oxford. The only deterrent to any action against Oxford was the queen herself. He knew of her great respect for Oxford's talents. On the other hand, Lady Burghley held a low opinion of her son-in-law. And, in time, Burghley's son Robert was to hate his brother-in-law even more than did his father. The reasons are complex but understandable. First of all, there was the middle class's natural jealousy of the old aristocracy. Burghley knew he was a newcomer to the nobility and even though he wanted to be part of the aristocracy, he looked down upon its members' improvident ways and superior airs. Even though his daughter's marriage had been arranged and almost forced upon Oxford, for many years he resented Oxford's lack of acquiescence in the matter. He could do little about it, however, for Oxford was under the protection of the queen. He was her favorite and, I am convinced, her lover.

Once his daughter died, some of the restraints disappeared. Almost immediately, he insisted on recouping the marriage fee, which, under the old feudal laws, he was in a position to collect. Prior to that, he had not mentioned the fee. He certainly didn't need the money. And he knew that Oxford was in financial straits.

There is no question that he and his family resented the allusions to him in the plays. They could hardly have passed unnoticed.

His plot was so successful in part because England was so

The First 1656 Drawing of the Shaksper Monument. Note that the hands are resting on a sack of grain.

closely controlled and tightly censored. Burghley decided to change the face of history so that the image of Burghley would remain a favorable one. The works of Oxford would be buried; a new author would be created. In effect, it was the greatest hoax in history—and it succeeded.

We need to know the ambiance in which this plot was nurtured, however.

The reader must understand three things about Elizabethan attitudes. As we have said, nobles were absolutely forbidden to attach their names to published plays or poems. A poet in those times, believe it or not, was considered by law to be in the same category as thieves and vagabonds. The author of *English Poesie* in 1589 stated that "poets are despised . . . subject to scorn and derision." Poets and poetry were scornfully regarded during the sixteenth century. However, self-styled noblemen poets were another thing, and copies of poems were passed among courtly friends. All actors were *legally* classified as rogues and vagabonds. Common people could attach their names to plays and poems, but not nobles.

Why? At that time, there were too many unemployed people in England. The dissolution of the monasteries by Henry VIII had thrown upon a high unemployment market many monks. The monasteries had been taking care of many homeless and starving people by running what today would be called soup kitchens. When the monasteries were abolished, most of these people became beggars. England was overrun by beggars, the sort of thing that is plaguing American cities today.

Graduates of Oxford and Cambridge could not find jobs, and, as a result, would recite poetry or try to amuse people whenever they could drum up a crowd. Following these recitals they would pass the hat around. This sort of thing is happening in Manhattan today, when students or performers try to eke out a living by putting on performances whenever the opportunity occurs. Hence in England, certain communities would enact strict laws limiting the activities of poets, rogues, and vagabonds. Unless they had a certificate showing they were members of a lord's company, actors were dealt with summarily. A person either had a regular occupation, such as farmer, woodworker, blacksmith, hatmaker, or tailor, or else he was considered a drifter and was shunted away from the particular community. Also, there were divisions among the employed population, and dress regulations were in force. Farmers, for instance, were required to wear blue clothing.

The second thing to understand is that Elizabethan England was a place of *absolute* censorship. Jail or death awaited anyone who dared to write anything against the queen or the government.

Finally, execution, either public or private, was much more common than it is today. There were so many plots and counterplots that those in power had to make sure that all possibility of treason was quickly smothered. Most of this plotting had a religious basis.

Having this in mind, we can understand better how the earl of Oxford could be involved in any plots swirling around in the queen's court. He was involved with the writing of plays and poetry, and this was taboo for a nobleman. But there is an additional aspect to this. He was pitted against the Puritans, who were tenaciously set against the theater and wanted to transform England into a pure Calvinistic state.

He was also for a time—certainly from 1570 to 1590, but with a period of banishment—a decided favorite of the queen, and there were a number of young bucks all hankering to take his place.

In his plays and in his poetry, he was fond of making fun of people, or uncovering their misdeeds. He does this with his own father-in-law.

In his chronicle plays especially, he comments on the political or international situation. A good example is *Richard II*, wherein he is really warning the queen to be on guard against treasonable plotting by some of her subjects.

He was briefly involved, as a person of Roman Catholic leanings, in the religious turmoil that plagues England.

He was a man of flesh and blood, and was certainly pursued by some of the ladies of the court. One of these, Anne Vavasor, was almost his undoing.

In addition to his illegitimate son by Anne Vavasor, he might have had another illegitimate son, and undoubtedly did. I believe that the earl of Southampton was his son. Or perhaps another one popped up somewhere to cause a court scandal.

Finally, and perhaps most important, Oxford may have com-

mitted the unpardonable sins of appearing—albeit incognito—as
an actor in his own plays, losing caste in doing so. In a poem by a
John Davies, officially registered in 1610, the following lines
appear:

> Hadst thou not played some kingly parts in sport,
> Thou hadst been a companion for a king;
> And been a king among the meaner sort.

He says so himself: "Alas, 'tis true! I have gone here and there,
and made myself a motley to the view."

Whatever opportunities there were for trouble abrewing, then
the seventeenth earl of Oxford, certainly was in the midst of it.

There are several theories as to why the earl of Oxford adopted
a nom de plume and how the Stratford man slid into the myth
that he was the real Shakespeare.

One could argue that Oxford got tired of the pirating of his
plays, since he could not sign his real name to them, and simply
assumed the pseudonym "William Shakespeare" or "Shakespeare" so that could have greater control. This, however, hardly
holds water.

It could also be that the Stratford man was dealing in pirated
plays while he was in London, and saw how easy it might be to
give people the impression that he was the author Shakespeare.

I think that the explanation is more complex. It was the culmi-
nation of all eight of the factors listed above. Things came to such
a point that the queen decided to do something. I can just imagine Burghley saying to the queen: "Your Majesty, matters have
reached a dangerous impasse. We have to solve this problem,
once and for all." Only, long-winded as he was, it would have
been a letter or speech twenty times as long. I can also imagine
the queen saying: "Oh, dear! How can we put an end to all this?"
It really doesn't matter who suggested the plot first.

What was the causal happening? We can only surmise. Perhaps
he wrote something that might be considered treasonable or that
might have serious international repercussions. Or, it could have
been, as I have said, the transgression of actually acting on stage.
I am convinced that Lord Burghley and his son, Robert, were the
prime instigators. I think that all the possibilities for trouble
combined to make it necessary to find a solution:

1. It wouldn't do to admit to the world that the earl of Oxford was the author of plays, sonnets, and other poems.
2. The enmity of other court figures grew into a problem for the queen, who was anxious to keep things peaceful.
3. The people alluded to in his plays wanted to put an end to Oxford's privileged stature.
4. The queen could not have Oxford involved in political matters.
5. The growing Puritan powers were out to "get" Oxford. After all, he was a prime personage of the despised theater.
6. Some of the court figures, especially relatives of Anne Vavasor, were also Oxford's enemies.
7. An illegitimate son may have made his position untenable.

So, four things had to be done. One, a name had to be created—William Shakespeare. Two, a different person had to be clothed in the name of this new creation. William Shaksper, being in London, seemed neatly suited for this ploy. Three, it was necessary to destroy all traces of the earl of Oxford. Four, Shaksper had to be given credibility as a writer.

All four things were done. Were relatives of the earl of Oxford involved in this plot? There is every reason to believe that they were, or at least that they knew about it. They must also have known of the merry pirating of Oxford's plays.

What happened to the original manuscripts? No one knows. It may be that they were destroyed in the famous fire that leveled the Globe Theater in 1613. Maybe they were secreted somewhere and will someday be found. I believe that Burghley and his son or perhaps the Puritans had them destroyed. The queen was too appreciative of Oxford's talents and too respectful of literary excellence to perform such a dreadful act. But Burghley and his son were in a position to carry through any plan they might have had.

When members of the family decided they could not let these plays be forgotten, they had difficulty in locating authentic, original copies. Mostly they found actors' copies and second or third pirated copies, with undecipherable words, errors, and changes. Thus came about one of the greatest scams in literary history.

Burghley, his son Robert, and the queen together must have made the decision to use William Shaksper of Stratford. Since

Shaksper could not write, there was no danger that he might write inferior material that would uncover the plot. They made sure that he returned to Stratford, and would be out of the way. We must remember that at that time, the town could just as well have been a thousand miles away. I am convinced that Southampton paid Shaksper one thousand pounds, which was a great deal of money in those days. But Shaksper was in a strategic position to exact a high toll. Curiously what he spent was roughly three-quarters of the one thousand pounds he was supposed to have received.

What role did the Stratford man play in the charades? Well, he certainly knew how to take care of himself. When he realized he was indispensable, he probably took full advantage of the situation, letting people believe he was Shakespeare. This attitude may have inspired Oxford. In *The Taming of the Shrew*, a sleeping beggar is dressed as a lord. Upon awakening, the beggar assumes that he *is* a lord.

It is not unnatural for a writer using a nom de plume to insert in his writings clues as to the real name, and this Oxford does in his plays. Along with the need to hide is the urge to tell the truth.

When Shaksper saw other people appropriating stage plays written by Oxford, did he see an opportunity to get into the racket? Or did he get in later, when the plays came out under the name "William Shakespeare?" Or was he merely a pawn in the plot to transfer the authorship of the plays from Oxford to another man?

Let us repeat three facts that may help in sorting out the mystery: (1) England, mainly London, was a relatively small place. It was easy to control things; (2) There were many reasons for concealing the authorship of Oxford; and (3) Burghley, his son Robert, and others could easily manage to control and censor.

To the above, we might add that political clout was working against Oxford. His in-laws were against him; the Puritans, whose power was ascending, were against him because he led the theater movement, which they believed to be an abomination of man. In addition, Hatton and perhaps other contenders for court importance were jealous of Oxford's position with the queen.

In such an inflammatory situation, the smallest irregularity could have caused the "scandal" that Oxford refers to, the blemish upon his name. What that scandal could have been, we don't know. Burghley's daughter, Oxford's wife, had died in 1588. Perhaps, at this point, Burghley was able to say, "Enough is enough! For the sake of the state, we must put an end to the earl of Oxford's disgraceful behavior." The queen may have countered that it would be wrong to keep a great mind from expressing itself in plays and poetry. A compromise may have been worked out. Let him write, but under a pseudonym.

9
A Hundreth Sundrie Flowres

In 1573, there was published *A Hundreth Sundrie Flowres*, the first anthology of poems in English literature.

Instead of an author's name, the posy "Meritum petere, grave" appeared. This is Oxford's posy, and he must have borne the expenses of printing. (A posy was an expression giving a clue to the real author.) The book contained forty-five poems credited to George Gascoigne; sixteen to "meritum petere, grave"; and seventeen to the posy "Si fortunatus infoelix." The last posy has been found to be that of Christopher Hatton, a commoner who had become a great favorite of the queen. While Hatton was away in Spa, near Liege in Belgium, sent there by the queen to recuperate from illness, the anthology was published. In it Hatton's affair with an "Elinor" was unfolded, thus endangering his attachment to the queen. The name "Elinor," beginning with an "E," may have been a thinly veiled substitute for Elizabeth, the queen herself.

As you can imagine, Hatton was furious, and yet he could say nothing, since any statement on his part would only give credence to the affair. In 1575, when Oxford left England for a military assignment on the continent, Hatton seized an opportunity for revenge.

A new edition of *Flowres* was quickly issued, with many changes by persons unknown. Now the credit for all the poems was attributed to Gascoigne. "The Adventures of Master F. I.," referring to Hatton, were completely done over in a new story, the "Fable of Ferdinando Ieronimi," supposedly a translation from the Italian by a fictitious author, "Bartello." There was even an added dig at Oxford with a poem on the theme, "War is Sweet to Those Who Know Nothing About It." How corny can you get? But such was the rivalry for the queen's favor. I am convinced that Hatton was one of Elizabeth's lovers. "My sheep," she called him.

The Later Version of the Monument. Now Shaksper has a quill pen in his hand.

Who can blame him for wanting to maintain a position of strength?

When Oxford returned from Europe, it was his turn to be furious. Remember he had also learned that his wife was supposed to have cuckolded him. You can imagine his mental state. Somehow, the remaining copies of *Flowres* were called in and confiscated by order of the queen's majesty commissioners. The queen held all the power, of course. She knew what it was all about. It was time to put a halt to all these shenanigans.

Moreover, the second edition of *Flowres*, in giving credit to George Gascoigne for all the poetry contained, enabled him to be boosted in court circles. The result was that Queen Elizabeth seriously considered appointing him poet laureate. This honor would have designated Gascoigne as the outstanding poet of the time, thus outshining the earl of Oxford. Those in the know were aware that Oxford's poetry was far superior to Gascoigne's. Queen Elizabeth never got around to actually designating Gascoigne as the poet laureate, but Oxford was greatly disturbed by the apparent put-down he suffered. Perhaps the queen was threatening to honor Gascoigne as poet laureate as a means of disciplining Oxford.

Incidentally, while Gascoigne was blamed for the first edition of *Flowres*, and for the temerity of being free with court favorites, he was never castigated openly. He apologized for having been involved, but in the byzantine relationships of court favorites, the matter was hushed up until the second edition came out.

Oxford had won the first round; Hatton the second. Oxford lamented visibly. In a poem signed "E. O.", he wrote:

> The more my plaints I do resound
> The less she pities me;
> The more I sought the less I found,
> Yet mind she meant to be.

At any rate, Gascoigne died in 1577, ending that episode in Oxford's files. The important thing to remember about this period is that Oxford was writing poetry and was active in the literary scene, even though such activity was hampered by court rules regarding the use of the noblemen's names.

TO.THE.ONLIE.BEGETTER.OF.
THESE.INSVING.SONNETS.
M^r.W.H. ALL.HAPPINESSE.
AND.THAT.ETERNITIE.
PROMISED.

BY.

OVR.EVER-LIVING.POET.

WISHETH.

THE.WELL-WISHING.
ADVENTVRER.IN.
SETTING.
FORTH.

T. T.

The Dedication Page of Shake-speare's Sonnets

10

Sonnets

Over a period of years, Shakespeare wrote 154 sonnets of a very personal nature. The title of the published collection is *Shakespeare's Sonnets*. Note the use of the hyphenated name which, in itself, denotes a pseudonym.

Contained in these sonnets, are references to the "Fair Youth," a person of noble station and of great beauty; and to a "dark lady" that the poet is infatuated with, and who is trying to lure the young man from him. Who are these two persons? I am convinced that the "Fair Youth" is the illegitimate son whom Oxford cannot acknowledge. I think he is Henry Wriothesley, third earl of Southampton. Oxford implores him to beget a family so that he may perpetuate himself. The sonnets are really Oxford's autobiography. It should be pointed out that the writer is speaking as if he were in loco parentis. One thing is certain: the tender emotions and sensitive phrases are hardly what the Stratford man, with his crude stance and background, would ever write.

In 1608 a Thomas Thorpe brought out this full collection of sonnets. No one knows how these poems came to him. Certainly, being dead, Shakespeare did not give them to him.

Do we have any clues? Yes. Let us remember that Shakespeare appends his name for the first time to a poem in 1593, and that the poem, *Venus and Adonis*, is dedicated to Henry Wriothesley, the third earl of Southampton. Then comes *The Rape of Lucrece*, and we note that in the dedication the terms used are similar to those in the sonnets.

If Southampton was Oxford's son, why even consider a marriage with Elizabeth Vere, Oxford's daughter and naturally, Southampton's half-sister? Simple. It was a secret that only Oxford and Southampton's mother knew. Note that the idea was dropped quickly enough—Elizabeth married the sixth earl of Derby. Theoretically, were Southampton not his son, he would have espoused his marriage to his daughter. But he talks about the many young ladies who would be fine for bearing his children. Either that, or Oxford held on to the idea that his wife, Anne, had cuckolded him, and had a daughter by someone else.

It is evident from the verses that the Fair Youth is a nobleman. As we read the sonnets, it is unthinkable that a commoner such as Shaksper could ever have dared to address them to a nobleman. Only another nobleman—in this case, Oxford—could have had the presumption to write in such terms to a fellow nobleman. The Fair Youth is the earl of Southampton. Sonnet 25 contains a revealing line:

> That every word doth almost tell my name.

In Sonnet 29, this line appears:

> I may not ever more acknowledge thee.

How clear it is! He can neither divulge his real name nor acknowledge his progeny.

In Sonnet 37, he writes:

> As a decrepit father takes delight
> To see his active child do deeds of youth,
> So I, made lame by Fortune's dearest spite,
> Take all my comfort of thy worth and truth.

Shakespeare (Oxford) is speaking in a fatherly tone, as a father. Also, the expression "made lame" refers to the unfortunate blow he received during his fighting with Knyvet.

As I said, the *Sonnets* are autobiographical. We find in them Shakespeare's attitude toward women. There is passionate tenderness and yet distrust. He admits to "vulgar scandal" and that his good name has been lost. What his vulgar scandal is, no one knows for sure.

Was it the affair with Anne Vavasor? Or was yet another affair? After all, Oxford was a handsome noble with the full powers of a vigorous man. The ladies would certainly swarm around him. Did the "vulgar scandal" refer, rather, to Oxford's acting on the stage, which was forbidden to a nobleman? Or did it concern his outspokenness about happenings or personages at court? When the *Sonnets* were published, the expression used in referring to the author was "our ever-living poet," which would indicate that the author was dead. The expression "ever-living" connotes someone who was well-known, but even though he may be dead, he is "ever-living."

Who is the person Shakespeare is talking to? It must be Henry Wriothesley, earl of Southampton. All the facts seem to fit. For instance, he says:

> You had a father. Let your son say so.

Evidently, the writer knew the young man's mother:

> Thou art thy mother's glass and she, in thee,
> Calls back the lovely April of her prince.

Note it couldn't have been Shaksper writing these lines. As a commoner, he couldn't address a noble person in such a familiar way.

In the verses, the author speaks of himself as an old man. At the time the *Sonnets* were written, Shaksper was about twenty-six. How could he be talking of himself as an old man, and urging another young man to marry?

In 1590, Oxford was forty years of age. Does the following line tie in with his age?

> When forty winters shall besiege thy brow,
> And dig deep trenches in thy beauty's field.

Above all, Oxford wanted his aristocratic line to continue. He had hd three daughters but no legitimate son.

The Stratfordians, in trying to explain the *Sonnets*, state that it was simply a literary exercise on the part of Shaksper. They are hard-pressed to explain the endearing phrases to the Fair Youth. A few say it's a case of outright homosexuality. Nonsense! You don't tell your homosexual lover to go have a family!

Another clue is the fact that the poems *Venus and Adonis* and *The Rape of Lucrece*, which are dedicated to Wriothesley, express the same ideas expressed in the *Sonnets*. The *Sonnets* were probably dedicated to Henry Wriothesley, the earl of South-ampton. The dedication page shows that they are dedicated to

"W. H.," a reversal of Wriothsley's initials, as was done from time to time.

The earl of Southampton received an education comparable to that of Oxford. Like Oxford, he was a Queen's Ward under the guardianship of Burghley. He was a student at Cambridge and at Gray's Inn. Unfortunately, he became involved in the rebellion of the earl of Essex against Queen Elizabeth. He could have been executed, as Essex was, but instead he was put into prison. When James I became king, one of his first acts was to free Southampton. Perhaps his special treatment points to his secret princely birth.

Like Oxford, Southampton had a deep interest in drama, and was a generous patron of poetry. In the case of the *Sonnets*, even a number of Stratfordians, mainly C. Stopes, Akrigg, and Rowse, agree that the Fair Youth is Southampton.

The secrets of the *Sonnets* will probably never be known by either side. The Freeman manuscript identifies Southampton as the queen's secret grandson (see Chapter 14). Such a scenario would shed light on Oxford's sonnets.

11
The Earl of Oxford in Italy

I have mentioned that in 1575, the earl of Oxford received permission from the queen to travel to Europe, and particularly to Italy. Oxford, like Queen Elizabeth, knew the Italian language. He had also read widely in Italian books and been involved with the publication of two important Italian books: *Il Cortegiano*, by Baldassare Castiglione, and *Comforte*, by Girolamo Cardano. Oxford undoubtedly paid for the publication of both books.

His interest in Italy went further than that, however. Many Englishmen were inspired by the Renaissance movement in the various Italian city-states. At that time, there was no unified Italy. That was not to come until 1870. But the economic and military importance of the various Italian city-states had led to extraordinary cultural development. New standards were created that have survived to this very day. At the time, England was coming out of its shell culturally and economically and, like Italy later on, was beginning to coalesce as a nation. In Italy, however, not one but a number of courts flourished: Venice, Florence, Palermo, Rome, Verona, Milan, Genoa, Turin, Pavia, Naples, Mantua, Pisa, and other lesser ones.

When Italy was finally unified in 1870, there were thirteen states or regions, just as there were in our own union in the eighteenth century. One reason a trip to Italy is so enlightening is that each town has its own flavor. At Urbino, the court had evolved a standard of knightly behavior that inspired Oxford. That is why he took such an interest in subsidizing *Il Cortegiano*. Both Oxford and Elizabeth wanted to establish the Italian courtly standard in London. Not so Burghley. Although he had one of the best libraries in England, he had no use for plays, poetry, or the more refined aspects of a cultural renaissance. Moreover, he was against Oxford going overseas.

Can you imagine how Oxford's spirits soared as he landed in

Sir Edward Vere. Illegitimate son of the earl of Oxford by Anne Vavasor. (By permission of Minos D. Miller, Sr. Trust.)

France and paid his first visit to the court of Henry III, the son of Catherine de Medici? Imagine how they welcomed him, especially since Queen Elizabeth had given the earl a letter of introduction, and since Catherine de Medici wanted to keep close relations with England as a political ploy against Spain. His next stop was Strasbourg, which was then a German city, where he went to converse in Latin with Johannes Sturmius. Sturmius had great influence on education in Europe and was rector of the university at Strasbourg. One can imagine the intellectual stimulus on young Oxford!

On he went to Italy. At the court in Venice, he was given another royal reception. The earl of Oxford was fascinated by Italy. Through his readings and then his visit, he found rich material for his tragedies and romantic comedies. Oxford had an appreciation for Italy second only to Dante. On his visit to Padua, which then belonged to the Republic of Venice, he wrote the following:

> For the great desire I had
> To see fair Padua, nursery of arts,
> I am arrived for fruitful Lombardy,
> The pleasant garden of great Italy. . . .

For instance, He knew of the intense rivalry between Siena and Florence. He used a phrase that is pure Italian: "The Florentines and the Sienese are (at each other) by their ears" ("si pigliano per gli orecchi"). Only a visitor would pick up so many small details.

Evidence of Oxford's command of Italian can be found in *Taming of the Shrew,* in which he includes lines of pure Italian:

Petruchio: Signior Hortensio, come you to part the fray?
  "con tutto il core, ben trovato," may I say.
Hortensio: "Alla nostra casa ben venuto, molto honorato signor mio, Petruccio."

There are slight differences in spelling because of the English usages, an example being "honorato" instead of "onorato."

While in Italy, the earl of Oxford was especially inspired by the commedia dell'arte. The mechanics of its stage presentations influenced the make-up and the technical aspects of his plays. Evident in the plays themselves was Oxford's enthusiasm for

Renaissance painters and sculptors. For instance, in *The Winter's Tale*, he mentions Giulio Romano, a remarkable sculptor *of that period*. Now where would Shaksper get a detail like that?

The influence of the commedia dell'arte is especially apparent in *Love's Labour's Lost*. How could Shaksper have even known about the commedia dell'arte? No commedia company visited England until 1577 or 1578. The Stratford man was then fourteen, and there certainly is no record of his being interested in writing. He was still helping his father in farming or butchering. In 1575, when Oxford had visited the court of Henry III of France, the royal entertainment included the commedia dell'arte.

What was the commedia dell'arte? Developed in Italy, it was simply a form of comedy in which the plot was written out but the dialogue improvised by the actors. There were certain stock characters, all masked, who appeared and reappeared in the various comedies.

George Lyman Kittredge of Harvard says that the influence of the commedia dell'arte is visible throughout the play, *Love's Labour's Lost*. Shakespeare's precise descriptions of scenes, laws, and customs in Italy point to the certainty of a personal visit, that of the earl of Oxford. The scenes in his comedies are purely Italian. The many precise details could have been observed only during a personal visit.

I consider the Italian experience of the earl of Oxford the most important aspect of the case against Shaksper of Stratford. There aren't any false notes or mysterious gaps in the results of the trip as reflected in his comedies, except one or two possible errors that occur with most authors. The main ones are easily explainable. For example, Shakespeare refers to a beach in Bohemia. Today, of course, there is none. But at that time, Bohemia stretched to the seacoast because it included the duchy of Austria. Oxford has Proteus travel from Verona to Milan by boat. At that time, there was a well-used system of canals between the two cities, since roads were not in use then, as they are today.

It isn't quite clear in what order he visited some of the towns. We do know he was a guest at the court of Sicily. When Oxford got there, Sicily was under the rule of Spain. But before that, it had boasted the most brilliant court of Europe. Its total economic activity had been greater than that of England. Let us not forget that two years before Normans took over England in 1066, they had practiced amphibian landing from the southern part of Italy, crossing over and taking over Sicily. The Norman court in Sicily, as in England, had been outstanding, and Oxford, whose family went back to these same Normans, must have reveled in seeing Norman architectural influences in Palermo. While he was in Palermo, Oxford even proposed a jousting tournament, but no one accepted the challenge.

Now, let us see which Shakespearean plays drew upon Italian authors. *Measure for Measure* comes from the sixteenth century writer, Giovambattista Cinzio. *The Merchant of Venice* is derived from *Il Pecorone* of Fiorentino (1558). *A Midsummer Night's Dream* was inspired partly by the writings of the Roman poet, Ovid. Let us not forget that Oxford had worked with his uncle, Arthur Golding, on the translation of Ovid. *Much Ado About Nothing* is straight out of Matteo Bandello, a fifteenth-century writer of novellas or tales. *The Taming of the Shrew* was based on Ariosto's *I Suppositi*. The basic plot of *All's Well That Ends Well* is taken from the ninth novella of the third day of Boccaccio's *Decameron*. The physician's orphan, Giletta, becomes Helena in the play. Helena's great regard for the King's Ward, Bertram, probably was inspired by the feelings of Anne Cecil for the royal ward, the earl of Oxford, who was to become her husband.

One of the most famous speeches in Shakespeare's plays describes the seven ages of man. Where did he get it? Well, in a cathedral in Siena, there are panels that depict the seven ages of man.

Oxford was so smitten with the splendor, art, and sophistication of Italy that when he returned to England, he dressed in the Italian fashion, becoming known as the "Italianate Englishman."

While in Italy, Oxford ran short of funds and borrowed money from a Baptista Nigrone. He had written to Lord Burghley, who was in charge of his estates, to forward some money. This he received in Venice from a Pasquino Spinola. You may remember that in *The Taming of the Shrew*, there is a Baptista Minola, the father of Katherine. Incidentally, the amount was five hundred crowns, the same amount provided by Adam for his and Orlando's expenses in *As You Like It*. Like all authors, the earl of Oxford filled his plays with various names and happenings in his own life.

In *As You Like It* occurs the sentence, "You have sold your own lands to see other lands". This clearly can only refer to Oxford's experience in selling a number of his estates in order to go to Europe. He traveled with a retinue of eight people, according to the standards of a nobleman. His retinue, according to Burghley, included two gentlemen, two grooms, one payend (a disburser of funds), a harbinger (an advance man, or someone who goes ahead to make arrangements); a housekeeper; and a trencherman (a cook).

Pietro Rebora in *L'Italia nella Dramma Inglese* says, "Shakespeare possessed a profound knowledge of the Italian language and culture of which he made an amazing use in his plays."

Oxford had a love for many Italian cities. In his book, *Shakespeare and Italy*, Professor Ernesto Grillo makes the following count of cities mentioned by Shakespeare in his plays: Italy, about 800 times; Rome, 400 times; Venice, 52; Naples, 34; Milan, 25; Florence, 23; Padua, 22; and Verona, 20. Genoa, Mantua, Pisa, Ferrara, and other cities are also mentioned frequently. Grillo continues, "When we consider the north of Italy, he [Shakespeare] reveals a profound knowledge of Milan, Bergamo, Verona, Mantua, Padua, and Venice . . . [and] derived his information from an actual journey through Italy and not through books." Wouldn't you say that Oxford was obsessed with Italy?

There is no doubt about it: names, characters, scenes, and entire plots are inspired from both his visit to Italy and also from Italian books that Oxford imported from Venice, Rome, and Florence. Remove the Italian influence from Shakespeare and there is little left besides the chronicle plays.

We know that the earl's father supported a company of players. The earl himself was involved with players' groups not only as a student at Gray's Inn but at the court, and later with his own groups. One can imagine how avid he was to see the various theater groups in Italy, their staging effects and mechanics. Let's face it. The earl of Oxford was *the* major force during the Elizabethan period in bringing the Renaissance from Italy into England.

In *Love's Labour's Lost*, Shakespeare quotes the well-known proverb:

> Venetia—Venetia
> Chi non ti vede, non to pretia
> (He who does not see you, cannot appreciate you.)

There are a number of other instances where he uses Italian words, and expressions and proverbs of Italian origin. For instance, "se fortuna mi tormenta, la speranza mi contenta" (If fortune torments me, hope satisfies me). A phrase such as "sound as a fish" comes from the Italian "sano come un pesce."

Giordano Bruno's influence can be discerned in Hamlet's soliloquy, "To be, or not to be," and also in Sonnets 106, 109, and 123. Giordano Bruno had been for several years lecturing at Oxford University in England. But the phrase, "to be, or not to be," can also be traced to Cardano's *Comforte*.

The famous line, "Who steals my purse steals trash . . . ," can be traced to Canto 51 of Berni's revision of *Orlando Innamorato*.

Note what Shakespeare says about travel:

> rather
> to see the wonders of the world abroad,
> than living dully sluggardised at home
> wear out thy youth with shapeless idleness.

Read the following lines from the same play. Oxford is certainly talking about himself:

> Twere good, I think, your lordship sent him thither:
> There shall be practice tilts and tournaments,
> Hear sweet discourse, converse with noblemen,
> And be in the eye of every exercise
> Worthy his youth and nobleness of birth.

In *Othello* Oxford alludes to his own noble birth:

> I fetch my life and being
> From men of royal siege, and my demerits
> May speak unbonneted to as proud a fortune
> As this that I have reached.

The same play contains references to Lady Oxford's rumored infidelity, which induced Oxford to spurn her publicly on returning to England from France. Burghley is Brabantio; Oxford, Othello; Lady Oxford, Desdemona; and Oxford's servant receiver, Iago. Desdemona says:

> Why do you weep?
> Am I the motives of these tears, my Lord?

If haply you my father do suspect,
An instrument of this your calling back
Lay not the blame on me.

(4.2.43–7)

When Oxford returned from Italy, just as some of us do when we return from a trip abroad, he brought gifts back. The main one would be for his queen who had given him permission to travel. She especially prized a pair of perfumed gloves trimmed with four tufts of roses of colored silk. She was painted for her portrait wearing those gloves.

All the evidence suggests that the writer of Shakespeare's comedies was a person of broad culture, extensive reading, and one who was familiar with Latin, Italian, and French. He certainly traveled in Italy. Even Grillo, who had been brought up in the Stratford tradition, felt that Shaksper must have traveled in Italy. The only flaw with that assumption is: (1) Shaksper wouldn't have had the money, and (2) even if by some miracle he had managed to get there, he would not have been received at the princely courts of Italy as a visiting nobleman of high rank.

When the Stratfordians run out of arguments, they always revert to the basic answer: Shaksper was a genius, and a genius can create anything. It seems to me a little naive, however, to expect the Stratford commoner, in the few years that we can possibly *assume* he was in London, to lose overnight his Warwickshire accent and vocabulary; learn Latin, Greek, Italian, and French; somehow latch on to the inner doings at court; dream up the vocabularies of royal sports; acquire a legal background; and then, after creating all of this by divine inspiration, decide to stop writing and resume the tawdry chores of his mediocre pre-London life.

It just doesn't add up.

12
Hamlet as an Example

Let us examine one play, *Hamlet*, to see how it dovetails with Oxford's life and also the happenings in England at the time. The same thing can be done with any of Shakespeare's works. The reader who wishes to delve further into such an analysis can read the chapters on *Hamlet* in *The Hidden Allusions in Shakespeare's Plays*, by Eva Turner Clark, and also *This Star of England*, by Dorothy and Charlton Ogburn. It won't be easy reading. A lot will be duplicative. and in some instances, there will be different interpretations.

To fully understand the allusions in Shakespeare, one must know about the court in Elizabethan England. England was really a small country, whose hub was London. And in London, the court was practically everything. Queen Elizabeth was imperious, fun-loving, cultured, and fond of intellectual activities. She wanted to serve her country well. She liked men, and enjoyed having her favorites. The earl of Oxford had been one, probably even her lover, even though he was much younger than she. Other favorites had been, at various times, Leicester, Hatton, Essex, and Raleigh. She relied on Burghley, but he was too stodgy to be a favorite in the romantic sense.

Her stance on religion was more complex. Elizabeth was a Protestant, and she observed the Protestant line because her country's diplomacy required it. But she was also somewhat Catholic in spirit, and liked certain aspects of Catholicism. Many of the nobles continued to practice Catholicism, a few of them plotting against the queen in an effort to replace her with Mary, Queen of Scots. So you see, Queen Elizabeth had a difficult path to follow.

Oxford, who was Catholic in spirit, had been drawn one of the Catholic plots, but when he realized it was against the queen, he withdrew. For this reason, and also because he had carried on an

Edward De Vere, Seventeenth Earl of Oxford

affair with Anne Vavasor, the queen confined him to the Tower. While there, Oxford could still write and be waited on. On 8 June 1593 he was released. All these bizarre relationships and happenings are alluded to in Shakespeare's plays.

Hamlet is full of allusions to court characters, especially to Burghley. He pokes fun at Leicester, referring to him as a peacock because he strutted about in court in elegant dress. He calls Hatton an ass.

Note what he says:

> A murderer and a villain;
> A slave that is not twentieth part the tithe
> of your precedent lord.

> (3.4.110–12)

Leicester is the murderer, because he is believed to have murderered his wife; Hatton is the villain; Raleigh is the slave; and Oxford, of course, is the precedent lord.

He also refers to Elizabeth:

> Frailty, thy name is woman!

> (1.2.152)

Why was the play set in Denmark? In 1583, Oxford's brother-in-law, Lord Willoughby, had been asked to confer the Order of the Garter on King Frederick of Denmark.

Prince Hamlet is a take-off on the earl of Oxford himself. Oxford's mother had married with "unseemly haste" after her husband's death. So had Queen Gertrude of Denmark.

In England, there was enmity between the earl of Leicester and the earl of Sussex. The play character Claudius, the King of Denmark, was inspired by Leicester.

Polonius is certainly modeled after Lord Burghley. Laertes, Polonius's son, is Burghley's son, Robert Cecil. Horatio is suggested by Sir Horatio Vere, Oxford's first cousin and close friend. The Ghost is the earl of Sussex. Queen Gertrude is a composite of Oxford's mother and Queen Elizabeth. In Ophelia, Oxford is really describing his wife, Anne Cecil. Old Fortinbras is really Mary Stuart, and here you must review the history of the imprisoned Mary, Queen of Scots. Young Fortinbras, the son, is really James I, son of Mary Stuart, and king of Scotland.

Clearly, Oxford got his ideas from events around him, and then patterned the characters of his plays after actual people on the scene. Could this have happened by chance? Hardly. Could it have happened to Shaksper of Stratford? Impossible. The Stratford man could neither have known all these court doings nor penetrated the queen's inner circles. Furthermore, as a commoner, he would have been severely punished had he dared to reveal any of these inner happenings. The Earl of Oxford, however, was premier lord of the realm. He had privileges. Furthermore, the queen respected him. Yet even he could not write under his own name. That is why he wrote his plays anonymously, at first, then under the pseudonym of Shakespeare or Shake-speare.

In the English court, as in all political settings, there was much jockeying for power. Oxford was unrivalled in terms of hereditary nobility. Even the queen could not boast as old a line of nobility as he had. But she had the ultimate power, and others—Burghley, Leicester, Hatton, and Raleigh—all tried to win her favor for their own ends. Oxford saw through their manipulations, and deplored the deceit, greed, and hypocrisy at court.

Oxford was disturbed by two other things: his mother's hasty marriage after the death of his father and to a worthless person; and Queen Elizabeth's loss of faith in him.

The play contains allusions to various events of the period. For instance, in 1582, there had been a plague. Referring to that event is the line ". . . and the sheeted dead, / Did squeak and gibber in the Roman streets." Referring to his own poor state of affairs in 1583, Oxford writes:

> How weary, stale, flat, and unprofitable
> Seem to me all the uses of this world!
>
> (1.2.139–40)

The precepts that Burghley gave to his son, Robert Cecil, as he was leaving for Paris, are uttered by Polonius:

> Be thou familiar but by no means vulgar
> The friends thou hast, and their adoption tried,
> Grapple them to thy soul with hoops of steel;
>
> . . . .
> This above all,—to thine own self be true;

And it must follow, as the night the day
Thou canst not then be false to any man.

(1.3.65–68, 82–84)

The gossip was that Leicester had used poison to get rid of people he didn't like, including his first wife, Amy Robsart. The Ghost is referring to that event when he tells Hamlet:

The serpent that did sting thy father's life
Now wears his crown.

(1.5.45–46)

In one scene Hamlet runs his sword through a spy who had been hiding behind the tapestry. I have already mentioned the real-life inspiration for that detail: While Oxford was a ward at the house of Burghley, he did the same thing to an under-cook who was spying on him from behind a tapestry. The man was undoubtedly spying for Burghley.

Another, more complicated parallel to events in *Hamlet* was the murder of Darnley (husband of Mary, Queen of Scots) by Bothwell, who was Mary's lover. Mary's son, who later became James I of England, naturally would want to avenge his father's murderer.

The King is afraid of coercing Hamlet, just as Leicester was afraid of avenging Oxford:

He's loved of the distracted multitude,
Who like not in their judgment, but their eyes.

(4.3.4–5)

It was the custom at one time in the Danish court to fire guns every time the king drank:

No jocund health that Denmark drinks today,
But the great cannon to the clouds shall tell.

(1.2.131–32)

Sometimes, Oxford uses the real names of characters. Rosencrantz and Guildenstern are two examples. His first cousins Horatio Vere and Francis Vere turn up in *Hamlet* as Horatio and Francisco. It is to Horatio that Hamlet pleads:

> O god, Horatio! What a wounded name,
> Things standing thus unknown, shall live behind me.
>
> (5.2.367–68)

This is a reference to the slander suffered by Oxford at the hands of his enemies. A relative accused him of being illegitimate. Many other disappointments and false accusations followed.

Let us remember that Oxford was getting poorer trying to serve the queen, keeping up an expensive lifestyle, and supporting fellow writers. He was forced to sell some of his estates. Meanwhile others, all upstarts, were getting rich from handouts in the court.

When Hamlet finds himself in financial straights, and has to cut down expenses, he laments his plight to Rosencrantz and Guildenstern:

> Beggar that I am, I am even poor in thanks.
>
> (2.2. 276)

Later on he says:

> I eat the air, promise-crammed; you cannot feed capons so.
>
> (3.2.95–96)

A reference to Oxford himself appears in a scene between Ophelia and Hamlet. Ophelia says to Hamlet:

> You are naught, you are naught.
>
> (3.2.150)

In other words, she says he is "0" (Oxford).

One troublesome aspect of Oxford's marriage was his wife's inability to break away from her father, who used his daughter to check up on his wayward son-in-law. Thus Polonius says:

> . . . in obedience hath my daughter shown me;
> And . . . had his solicitings
> All given to mine ear.
>
> (2.2.125–28)

We know that Oxford held the precepts of Castiglione—honor and valor above all other things—in high esteem. Burghley, in a letter to his son, pooh-poohs this ideal, admonishing, "Beware thou spendest not more than three or four parts of thy revenue. . . ." Thus, he would disapprove of Oxford's habit of spending more than his income and then having to sell off some of his property.

Oxford is really making fun of his father-in-law with the famous phrase "to thine own self be true." He is accusing Burghley of looking after his own interests.

We have copies of Burghley's long-winded letters to the queen. Oxford had takeoffs on this in the verbose letters of Polonius. Burghley knew his son-in-law was spoofing him in his plays, especially in the character of Polonius in *Hamlet*, and later on in Shylock in *The Merchant of Venice*. Can you blame him if he made sure that all files regarding Oxford disappeared? How did the queen react to all this? While she appreciated the efforts of Burghley to help her and, in fact, needed his support, she could appreciate the humor of it all. Burghley must have spoken to the queen about Oxford's pranks:

> Look you lay home to him;
> Tell him his pranks have been too broad to bear with,
> And that your Grace hath screen'd and stood between much heat and
> him.
>
> (3.4.1–4)

Oxford had thought of retiring to one of his estates, Wivenhoe, but Queen Elizabeth dissuaded him. She liked to have her chief dramatist around. In *Hamlet*, the King voices similar sentiments:

> For your intent
> In going back to school in Wittenburg,
> It is most retrograde to our desire:
> And we beseech you, bend you to remain
> Here in the cheer and comfort of our eye,
> Our chiefest courtier, cousin and our son.
>
> (1.2.118–23)

When Hamlet says to Ophelia

> I did love thee once.

This is exactly the feeling Oxford had for his child-wife, Anne.

He was always unsure whether her loyalty wasn't primarily to her father.

The following quote may sound meaningless, but it isn't if you know Oxford's life:

> I am mad north-north-west: when the wind is
> southerly I know a hawk from a handsaw.
> (2.2.388–89)

Oxford made a profitless investment in a company formed to find a northwest passage to Asia. The second part brings out Oxford's knowledge of falconry. (A handsaw is a heron.)

As we read and reread Shakespeare, we realize how sensitive a person he was. He invented many words, words that have now entered the English language. Some words had a meaning in the sixteenth century but are now almost unknown. In some cases, experts on Shakespeare differ as to the meaning of certain words ·or expressions. Let us not forget that Shakespeare had to write out his plays with an old-fashioned quill pen, which had to be sharpened from time to time. Blots of ink obscured the page, and often the printer could not decipher a certain word. But note the expressions from *Hamlet* that have become part of our everyday use. I'm citing only thirteen. There are far more:

(Hamlet)	"Frailty, thy name is woman!" (1.2.152)
(Polonius)	"Neither a borrower nor a lender be." (1.3.75)
(Marcellus)	"Something is rotten in the state of Denmark." (1.4.90)
(Polonius)	"Brevity is the soul of wit." (2.2.96)
(Queen)	"More matter, with less art." (2.2.95)
(Hamlet)	"Words, words, words." (2.2.93)
(Hamlet)	"There is nothing either good or bad but thinking makes it so." (2.2.250–1)
(Hamlet)	"What a piece of work is man!" (2.2.319)
(Hamlet)	"To be or not to be, that is the question." (3.1.64)
(Hamlet)	"Thus conscience does make cowards of us all." (3.1.84)
(Hamlet)	"Get thee to a nunnery." (3.1.122)
(Queen)	"The lady doth protest too much, methinks." (3.2.243)

(Osric)	"A hit, a very palpable hit." (5.2.282)
(Horatio)	"Good night, sweet prince,
	and flight of angels sing thee to thy rest!"
	(5.2.261–62)

Shakespeare is modern indeed!

Hamlet is autobiographical, of course. In Oxford's own life, his stepfather had usurped his mother's love and had taken over what estate was left to her—the same situation as in *Hamlet*, the estate being the kingdom itself. In both cases, there has been "unseemly haste":

> The funeral baked meats
> Did coldly furnish forth the marriage tables.
>
> (1.2.189–90)

Oxford disliked politicians, lawyers, and landdealers—base people whose tawdry grasping offended his feudal ideals.

My good lord, hauinge loked for yowre L. letters a greate while, atlength
when I grew to dispaire of them I receiued two from yowre L.
the pakets whiche at sundrie times I had sent this summer
towards England returned bake againe, by reason the place
being in the passages, none were suffred to pass but as
they came were returned bake, whiche I cam not to the
knowlege of till my returne now to Venice, where I haue
bene grieued withe a feuer, yet withe the help of god now
I haue recouerd the same and am past the dainger therof thoughe
browght veri weake therby, and hindred from a great deale of
trauell, whiche grieues me most, seminge my time not sufficient
for my desire, for althoughe I haue sene so mucke as sufficeth
one, yet wowld I haue tim: to profite therby, yowre L.
semes desirous to know how I leake Italy, what is myne
intention in trauell, and when I meane to returne, for my
lekinge of Italy, my lord I am glad I haue sen: it, and
I care not euer to se see it any more unles it be to
serue my prince or contrie, for myne intention to trauell
I am desirows to se moor of Germonie, wherfore I shall
desire yowre L. withe my lord of Leicster, to procure
me the next summer, to continue my licence, at the end
of whiche I meane undoubtedly to returne, I thought
to haue sene spaine, but by this, I gess the worse,
I haue sent on of my seruant into England withe sume
new disposition of my thinges there, wherfore I will
not troble yowre L. in this letter with the same, if this
siknes had not happend unto me whiche hathe taken
away this chifest time of trauell, at this present I wowld
not haue writtin for furthor leaue, but to supply this
whiche, I dought not her maiestie will not denie one so
small a fauour, by reason of my great charges of trauell

                                                    tom y L.

A Letter of the Earl of Oxford. Note the careful calligraphy.

13
The Letters of the Earl of Oxford

One great source of information regarding the character of Oxford's writing are some fifty letters that he wrote to various people, but mostly to his father-in-law and brother-in-law. As a matter of fact, one writer, William Plumer Fowler, in his book, *Shakespeare Revealed in Oxford's Letters*, shows convincingly that thirty-seven of the letters parallel his plays and sonnets as far as subject matter, vocabulary, certain thoughts, and special expressions. Burghley, in trying to censor and destroy all references to his son-in-law, could not achieve perfect results. The letters that survived show the similarity of vocabulary and expressions to the poetry of Oxford. The book also includes some facsimiles of letters written by Edward de Vere. This is important because careful calligraphy is in itself another proof that the true Shakespeare could not have been Shaksper of Stratford. Of the latter we have not a single letter. Moreover, half of the Oxford letters were written before the Stratford man was eleven! Most of the letters are in the British Library in London.

Was there perhaps another reason some of the letters survived? Destroying *all* letters might in itself have given the plot away. Burghley may have decided to leave some letters around. None of the letters are to his disadvantage, some are quite the opposite. They seem to say, "Look how careful I am of my son-in-law's interests, and look how irrational he is in some of his ideas." One refers to Oxford's willingness to exchange a one thousand-pound annuity for five thousand pounds in cash.

In history, there are many examples of cover-ups. The relationship of the earl of Oxford to Queen Elizabeth is one of them. Although the queen was seventeen years older than he was, she apparently became his mistress. In 1574, she dismissed her ministers and disappeared in the vicinity of Bristol. About eight months before that, the countess of Southampton had given birth to a child, who apparently had died. The queen's child by Oxford was substituted for the countess's child. Such an intrigue could account for the references to the "little western flower" in *A Midsummer Night's Dream* (I, 1, 166) and form yet another reason for concealing the authorship of the plays. This illegitimate son was then legitimized as the earl of Southampton (Henry Wriothesley). Could that child have been sired by Oxford? Some students of Shakespeare are sure of it, principally Mrs. Dorothy Ogburn. If this were so, then it provides the identity the Fair Youth.

Let us remember that it could have been possible for the queen to marry the earl of Oxford, since his royal antecedents were much older than hers. But the queen felt that because of patriotic reasons, it was important to preserve her image as the "Virgin Queen."

In 1586, the queen granted to the earl of Oxford a yearly sum of one thousand pounds an enormous sum. One of the conditions for this grant apparently, was that under no circumstances could the earl append his own name to any plays or poems. Throughout his verses, however, Oxford showed a desire to make his name known. He resorted to cryptic references such as "ver"; "O," for Oxford; "Ever," for E. Vere. He craved recognition, even though he was severely bound by authority not to reveal his name.

Let us repeat that there was an insistent effort by Philip II to make England into a Catholic state. There was a steady campaign to have Mary, Queen of Scots, take over the throne of England, and his effort persisted until Queen Elizabeth put her own relative to death. It became almost a state policy to make sure Oxford was put under wraps, so to speak. The idea of using Shaksper to muddy the issue was concocted and frozen into credibility. Even Ben Jonson, who makes fun of the Stratford Shaksper in two of his plays, lends himself to the ploy.

The role of Ben Jonson is a curious one. He knew what Shaksper was doing, and describes the imposter in his play, *Every Man Out of His Humour:*

> An essential clown, brother to Sordido, yet so enamoured of the name of a gentleman, that he will have it, though he buys it. He comes up every term to learn to take tobacco, and see new motions.

He is in his kingdom when he can get himself into company where he may be well laughed at.

Shaksper, in the character of Sogliardo, describes himself:

Nay, look you, Carlo; this is my humour now! I have land and money, my friends left me well, and I will be a gentleman whosoever it cost me.

In Shaksper's will, someone added a phrase to buy two rings for fellow actors Heminge and Condell. Then the statue of Shaksper, whose hands rested on a sack of grain, was changed to make him look like a writer. The sack of grain became a sheet of paper.

Oxford tried to get the queen to legitimize her son, Southampton, and make him her successor, which he had every right to be. Instead, the queen chose James of Scotland, the son of Mary, whom she had finally ordered to be beheaded.

The earl of Oxford, in a sad sacrifice for the good of his country, was forced to hide his own name and allow a Stratford man to assume the identity of Shakespeare.

Out of the hundreds of examples available in Fowler's book, I shall cite five:

"ill bestowed"

Much Ado About Nothing	3.2.100
Troilus and Cressida	2.2.159
Timon of Athens	4.3.461
Hamlet	2.2.547

"beam" in the sense of blinding beam
(Letter to the Lord Treasurer)

Comedy of Errors	3.2.56
Henry VI, Part 1	1.1.10

"worst" (Oxford letter from Venice to Burghley)

Merchant of Venice	1.2.95
King John	4.2.135
	4.3.27
Sonnet 92	line 5

"shadow and substance"
(Oxford's letter to Burghley on release from Tower)

Richard II	2.2.14–23
Henry IV, Part 2	3.2.126–31
Henry VI, Part 1	2.3.36–63
	5.4.133–35
Henry V, Part 2	1.1.13
Richard III	5.3.215
Two Gentlemen of Verona	4.2.121–27
Merry Wives of Windsor	2.2.207
Titus Andronicus	3.2.80
Sonnet 37	
Sonnet 53	
Merchant of Venice	3.2.127–29

"as firm as the law can make it"
(Oxford's Cannon Row letter)

Measure for Measure	2.4.94
Hamlet	1.1.87
Cymbeline	2.2.40

Fowler includes a summary table linking the vocabulary, expressions, and thoughts of Oxford's letters and Shakespeare's plays and sonnets. The almost complete similarity of these elements is probably the greatest proof that the earl of Oxford and Shakespeare were one. The correspondence between the two is just too overwhelming to be coincidental.

On the side of the earl of Oxford, then we have a preponderance of evidence. On the side of the Shaksper of Stratford, no evidence exists—nothing—nescience.

14

The Freeman Manuscript

While I was writing this book, a strange thing happened. The president of Fairleigh Dickinson University, Dr. Robert H. Donaldson, sent me a manuscript by Dr. Walter Freeman, a professor of literature who had passed away in 1974. It had been written about 1950. When Freeman passed away, his manuscript came into the hands of his son, who in turn passed it on to an alumna of Fairleigh Dickinson, Mrs. Carolyn Goff (née Richter), who lived in Arizona. Mrs. Goff, as a student at Fairleigh Dickinson, had been a close friend of the Freemans. When Dr. Donaldson was in Arizona at an alumni banquet, Mrs. Goff decided to give the manuscript to him. Dr. Donaldson, knowing of my interest in the earl of Oxford, passed it on to me.

As I read the manuscript, I realized it was a blockbuster. There were some errors in it; there were certain aspects that needed more research, but the manuscript haunted me. At this writing, I am still wondering about it, but one thing is sure; it does hang together in a rational way. If it is true, it answers a lot of questions. At any rate, this is how Dr. Freeman develops the Shakespeare enigma.

Shortly after Henry VIII died and while Mary Tudor was queen, Henry's last wife, Catherine Farr, married the earl of Seymour. Henry's daughter Elizabeth, as a royal princess, was ordered to be brought up in the Seymour home. Elizabeth was then sixteen. Lord Seymour took a great fancy to the royal princess, and used to love to play and frolic with her, when she was in bed, no less. He knew, of course, that someday she might become queen. At first, Lady Seymour looked upon such antics as harmless. After a while, it began to disturb her. Her instincts were right: The young princess was soon pregnant with a son. Lord Seymour was condemned to death for royal transgression,

The Duc d'Alençon. From the miniature by Nicholas Hilliard bound in Queen Elizabeth's little prayer book.

although the reason given was otherwise. Now, what to do with the illegitimate child?

As was the custom in those days, an illegitimate child of importance was brought up in a different home, in this case, that of Edward Stanley, earl of Derby. The boy had, at this point, the name of William Stanley.

As the certainty of Elizabeth's becoming queen of England became apparent, however, the child had to have a better title. After all, as the son of Elizabeth, who would become queen after Mary's death, he could possibly become king. Soon after her coronation in 1558, and after a visit to the home of the sixteenth earl of Oxford at Hedingham Castle, Elizabeth arranged for Arthur Golding, an outstanding scholar, to be the child's tutor. Golding, in 1561, prepared the will of the earl of Oxford, falsely naming the boy as the earl's son and heir. That child eventually became the seventeenth earl of Oxford.

If this is true, then it would explain why Oxford was such a favorite of Queen Elizabeth. It was simply a case of a mother being proud of her son. It also explains why she was so patient with him.

As queen, she arranged for him to marry the daughter of her loyal minister, William Cecil. Since the law prohibited marriage between commoner, and a noble, she ennobled Cecil by making him Lord Burghley. When the sixteenth earl of Oxford died, the heir, as ward of the Crown, was placed with William Cecil, who was charged with his guardianship. It was an ideal arrangement. The queen knew her son was in good hands, and since he lived nearby, she could see him as often as she wanted.

Incidentally, Dr. Freeman claims that Lady Stanley, the daughter of Edward Stanley, sued to have the seventeenth earl of Oxford declared illegitimate. As can be imagined, the case was hushed up by the queen and Lord Burghley and settled out of court.

Now begins the second part of this story. In 1565, the young earl of Oxford became enamored of a beautiful lass, Mary Browne, whose father was Viscount Montague. The father was not impressed with young Oxford, and forced his daughter to marry the second earl of Southampton while Oxford was away at Cambridge. This phase of his life may have inspired *Romeo and Juliet*. Oxford, thoroughly miserable, poured out his feelings in the poems he included in *A Hundreth Sundrie Flowres*, the first anthology of poems in English literature.

Dr. Freeman dwells on the role of the Puritans in the Shakespeare question. Indeed, the growing power of the Puritans played an important part, not only in the events of England during that time but also in the roles of playwrights. He also points out that one reason Queen Elizabeth vacillated so much in seeking a husband was that she wanted to leave the way open for her son, the earl of Oxford, to succeed her. All this while a great secret weighed upon a heavy heart—a secret son she could not acknowledge—a secret that probably only Burghley knew. Can one wonder why she did not want her son running off to war and risking death?

In the meantime, Oxford kept up his attention to Mary Browne, now Lady Southampton. After all, her marriage hadn't been a very happy one. She and Oxford were deeply in love. In 1573, she gave birth to a son, Henry Wriothesley—but it was Oxford's son. That is why he dedicated the *Sonnets* to W. H. (Henry Wriothesley's initials, reversed), thus to conceal Southampton's illegitimacy. If we accept Dr. Freeman's thesis, then the mystery of the *Sonnets* is solved. We know that they were dedicated to the love child he had by Mary Browne.

About this time, Oxford learned of his own illegitimacy. It was a great blow to him, but at the same time he realized how important a person he was as the queen's son. This secret gave him the fortitude to fight against his enemies.

Oxford petitioned Queen Elizabeth to recognize Mary Browne's son as his, which she secretly did, and agreed to leave the child in Mary's custody. Thus, Elizabeth, Oxford, and Henry Wriothesley were mother, son, and grandson. Indeed, the Ditchley portrait painted in 1592 shows the three together.

Now comes the most fantastic part of Dr. Freeman's thesis. It is really the story of Oxford's undoing by the Puritans, who were out to destroy him for his treasonable plays, especially *Richard II* and Richard III. The Puritans, we must remember, were violently opposed to the theater, and Oxford was a symbol of that institution.

They charged Oxford with treasonable writing. The punishment for that offense was death, and there seemed to be no question but that he would be found guilty by the Puritan-controlled Star Chamber. Oxford's family refused to accept his death as inevitable. It is at this point that they approached William Shaksper of Stratford, who was in London as a servitur in theater circles, and proposed to him that he testify that he had written the offensive plays. The similarity of the names made this ploy possible.

The price had to be significant enough to induce Shaksper to take the risk of losing his head, hence, the greatly-exaggerated payment of one thousand pounds. At the time, Shaksper was living in squalid circumstances and being fined as a tax defaulter. It was a chance of a lifetime.

Dr. Freeman claims that the proof is available in the Northumbrian Manuscript in Alnick Castle in Northumberland, in a bundle of Bacon's papers. It was Shaksper's perjured testimony that allowed the judges to reduce Oxford to a nobody without killing him. Why didn't they order Shaksper's death? He was a person of no importance.

Shaksper, with one thousand pounds in his possession, scampered off to Stratford to enjoy his newfound wealth. He bought the "second-best" house in town. He even had the gall to ask the College of Heralds for a coat-of-arms. Ben Jonson, in one of his plays, states that he paid for this privilege. Shaksper lied according to the agreement forged in court, insisting on the right to all the plays Oxford had in his possession. Reluctantly, Oxford gave him some older plays that had been gathering dust.

At the trial, the charges were also made that Oxford had been trying to turn a "Baronet into a king," in other words, had lusted for a succession to the Crown. In the end, he was completely stripped of any importance.

Now comes the last and most impressive chapter of this strange story. When Queen Elizabeth died and was succeeded by James I, some people were hostile to the former king of Scotland. Oxford shared this covert anti-James sentiment. James I knew of his stance but was afraid to punish Oxford, fearing an open rebellion. Oxford was, however, confined to the Tower at this time. But Oxford's son-in-law, the earl of Derby, suggested a compromise to King James. Since Oxford was the leading writer of England, he should be allowed to live and write. If he were removed from public sight, he would no longer be a threat to the king. James then gave Oxford a choice: death or oblivion. It was thus arranged that Oxford be spirited out of the Tower, and proclaimed to be dead—this happened in 1604, the official date of his death. To honor his "death," eight of his plays would be presented at court. Oxford was sent to the Isle of Man which, curiously, belonged to the Derby family. There he spent the rest of his life in utter isolation, attended to by one person only, who brought him food and water and logs for the fireplace. Oxford kept on writing and revising his plays until his actual death in 1611. It was then that King James had eight more of his plays presented at court—the last secret but open gesture to England's greatest poet.

Soon after his death, a group of Oxford's friends began to collect his plays, fearing that the Puritans would destroy them. This group, called the Grand Possessors, was headed by the earl of Pembroke and the earl of Montgomery, both related to Oxford. The earl of Southampton later joined the group. Ben Jonson was hired to edit the plays. To have them published they needed official permission which King James gave provided they were not published under the author's real name. His orders were carried out by the Puritan censors. It is at this time that the so-called Shakespeare monument was erected in Stratford, to further promote the Shakespeare scam. Jonson almost got away with putting a real likeness of Oxford on the volume, but the censors forced him to get an unknown artist, Droeshut, to fashion an inane, distorted drawing of "Shakespeare."

Thus ends Dr. Freeman's presentation. What is my reaction?

1. First of all, his presentation isn't one tenth as fantastic as the Stratfordians' case for Shaksper.
2. There are many parts that I accept because they agree with the case as presented by the Oxfordians.
3. I know how meticulous a scholar Dr. Freeman was. He must have had supporting evidence for his claims. Unfortunately, it is not included in the manuscript. At this writing, I have not succeeded in locating Dr. Freeman's son to see whether he might still have some of his father's papers. I have heard from the lawyer who handled the estate, and he has promised me he will look for Dr. Freeman's papers, which are in storage.
4. I have made arrangements to leave copies of Dr. Freeman's

manuscript in the library of Fairleigh Dickinson University, so that interested scholars can refer to it. Also, a copy has been deposited in the Rutherford Free Public Library in Rutherford, New Jersey.

The Freeman manuscript brings out an important aspect of the Shakespeare question—the necessity for continuing research—not to build up more assumptions for the Stratford man but to dig into the life of Edward de Vere, seventeenth earl of Oxford, whose papers, references, traces were blatantly destroyed by the Burghley plot.

15

Examples

In this chapter I cite, almost at random, fifteen examples from the plays or sonnets that parallel events in Oxford's life.

In Sonnet 36, Shakespeare is speaking to his illegitimate son, whom he does not acknowledge:

> Yet doth it steal sweet hours from love's delight.
> I may not evermore acknowledge thee,
> Lest my bewailed guilt should do thee shame;
> Nor thou with public kindness honour me,
> Unless thou take that honour from thy name:
> But do not so; I love thee in such sort,
> As, thou being mine, mine is thy good report.

In Sonnet 71, he is warning his son to forget him lest he harm himself:

> No longer mourn for me when I am dead
> Than you shall hear the surly sullen bell
> Give warning to the world that I am fled
> From this vile world, with vilest worms to dwell:
> Nay, if you read this line, remember not
> The hand that writ it; for I love you so,
> That I in your sweet thoughts would be forgot,
> If thinking on me then should make you woe.
> O, if, I say, you look upon this verse
> When I perhaps compounded am with clay,
> Do not so much as my poor name rehearse;
> But let your love even with my life decay;
> Lest the wise world should look into your moan,
> And mock you with me after I am gone.

Oxford, in an attempt to rebuild his finances, owed a Mr. Lock three thousand pounds that he had invested in the Frobisher expedition to find a northwest passage, and also to find valuable ores. This excerpt is from *The Merchant of Venice*:

Shylock. Three thousand ducats,—well.
Bassanio. Ay, sir, for three months.
Shylock. For three months,—well.
Bassanio. For the which, as I told you, Antonio shall be bound.
Shylock. Antonio shall become bound,—well.
Bassanio. May you stead me? Will you pleasure me? Shall I know
  your answer?
Shylock. Three thousand ducats for three months, and Antonio
  bound.

(1.3.1–7)

Oxford was a sympathizer of the Lancastrians and, indeed, members of his family had been leaders for their cause. Below is one of the many examples in which this sympathy is demonstrated. It is from *Richard III:*

Stanley. What men of name resort to him?
Christopher. Sir Walter Herbert, a renowned soldier;
  Sir Gilbert Talbot, Sir William Stanley;
  Oxford, redoubted Pembroke, Sir James Blunt,
  And Rice ap Thomas, with a valiant crew;
  And many others of great name and worth.

(4.5.8–13)

Note this parallel use of expressions. In an early poem by Oxford, the following occurs:

Patience perforce is such a pinching pain.

In *Romeo and Juliet:*

Patience perforce . . . makes my flesh tremble.

(1.5.88–89)

We know that Oxford received the queen's permission to travel in Europe, and that he had to sell some of his estates to pay for the expenses of his trip. Note the following excerpt from *As You Like It* (4.1.18-28):

Jaques. And, indeed, the sundry contemplation of my travels
  in which my often rumination wraps me in a most
  humorous sadness.
Rosalind. A traveller! By my faith, you have great
  reason to be sad: I fear you have sold

your own lands to see other men's;
    then to have seen much, and to have nothing,
    is to have rich eyes and poor hands.
Jaques. Yes, I have gained my experience.
Rosalind. And your experience makes you sad; I had rather
    have a fool to make me merry than experience to
    make me sad: and to travel for it too.

In a poem with the posy "Meritum petere, grave," Oxford refers to the heraldic colors of Queen Elizabeth, black and white. These were the heraldic colors of virginity and, as we know, Queen Elizabeth was intent on being known as the "Virgin Queen."

When first I thee beheld in colors black and white,
Thy face in form well framed with favour blooming still:
My burning breast in care did choose his chief delight,
With pen to paint thy praise, contrary to my skill,
Whose worthiness compared with this my rude devise,
I blush and am abash'd, this work to enterprise.

The affair between Queen Elizabeth and Oxford is part of history. So is her attachment to Leicester. In *A Midsummer Night's Dream*, the following dialogue between Oberon (Oxford) and Titania (Queen Elizabeth) describes their reconciliation after the banishment of Oxford. Leicester (Theseus) is supposed to have had Lord Sheffield done away with so that he could secretly marry Lady Sheffield just before their child was born. The queen and Oxford chide each other:

Oberon. Ill met by moonlight, proud Titania.
Titania: What! jealous Oberon. Fairies, skip hence:
    I have forsworn his bed and company.
Oberon. Tarry, rash wanton! am I not thy lord?
Titania. Then I must by thy lady; but I know
    When thou hast stol'n away from fairy land,
    And in the shape of Corin sat all day,
    Playing on pipes of corn, and versing love
    To amorous Phillida . . .
. . . .
Oberon. How canst thou thus for shame, Titania,
    Glance at my credit with Hippolyta,
    Knowing I know thy love to Theseus?
    Didst thou not lead him throught the glimmering night
    From Perigouna, whom he ravished?

And make him with fair Æglé break his faith,
With Ariadne, and Antiopa?

(2.2.60 et seq.)

Note this example from *Othello*, which like *Hamlet*, is one of Oxford's most autobiographic plays. It portrays the plea of Oxford's wife, Anne, for her husband to trust her and to come back to her. In December 1581, Lady Oxford (Anne) had written a heartbroken letter to her husband expressing the very same thoughts.

Desdemona. O good Iago,
   What shall I do to win my lord again?
   Good friend, go to him: for, by this light of heaven,
   I know not how I lost him. Here I kneel:
   If e'er my will did trespass 'gainst his love,
   Either in discourse of thought or actual deed,
   Or that mine eyes, mine ears, or any sense,
   Delighted them in any other form;
Or that I do not yet, and ever did,
   And ever will, though he do shake me off
   To beggarly divorcement, love him dearly,
   Comfort forswear me! Unkindness may do much;
   And his unkindness may defeat my life,
   But never taint my love.

(4.2.148 et seq.)

In *Cymbeline* there is a reference to two villains. I have explained how Oxford, who had Catholic leanings, laid bare the plot of Henry Howard and Charles Arundel to do away with Queen Elizabeth and put Mary of Scotland in her place. The two villains are Howard and Arundel. When Shakespeare says he was "confederate with the Romans" he means he was (unwittingly) lending himself to the Roman Catholic cause.

Belarius. My fault being nothing,—as I have told you oft,—
   But that two villains whose false oaths prevail'd
   Before my perfect honour, swore to Cymbeline
   I was confederate with the Romans; so
   Follow'd my banishment.

Read Sonnet 108. Oxford is talking to his illegitimate son, whom he may not acknowledge. It is difficult, nay impossible to explain this sonnet in the Stratfordian sense. There is no problem when the Fair Youth is interpreted as Oxford's son:

> What's in the brain, that ink may character,
> Which hath not figured to thee my true spirit?
> What's new to speak, what new to register,
> That may express my love, or thy dear merit?
> Nothing, sweet boy; but yet, like prayers divine,
> I must each day say o'er the very same;
> Counting no old thin old, thou mine, I thine,
> Even as when first I hallow'd thy fair name.
> So that eternal love in love's fresh case
> Weighs not the dust and injury of age,
> Nor gives to necessary wrinkles place,
> But makes antiquity for aye his page;
> Finding the first conceit of love there bred,
> Where time and outward form would show it dead.

In a poem, "Love thy Choice" and signed "Earle of Oxenforde", Oxford reveals how the queen had engendered in him the feelings for love and passion, for grace, for primacy in courtly tournaments. This was one of the early and few poems in which Oxford had signed his name, a blemish on court protocol.

> Who taught thee first to sigh, alas, my heart;
> Who taught thy tongue the woeful words of plaint?
> Who filled your eyes with tears of bitter smart;
> Who gave thee grief and made thy joys to faint?
> Who first did paint with colours pale thy face?
> Who first did break thy sleeps of quiet rest?
> Above the rest in Court who gave thee grace?
> Who made thee strive in honour to be best?
> In constant truth to bide so firm and sure,
> To scorn the world regarding but thy friends?
> With patient mind each passion to endure,
> In one desire to settle to the end?
> Love then thy choice wherein such choice thou bind,
> As nought but death shall ever change thy mind.

In The Tempest, Oxford refers to the Duke of Alençon as "this mis-shapen knave" because of his revolting appearance. He hated his mother, Catherine de Medici, and refers to her as a witch. To "control the moon" means that Catherine was able to put pressure on Elizabeth. The phrase "flows and ebbs" meant simply that Elizabeth had to change her willingness to marry Alençon.

This mis-shapen knave,-
His mother was a witch; and one so strong
That could control the moon, make flows and ebbs,
And deal in her command without her power.

(5.1.268–71)

In *Troilus and Cressida*, there is a reference to the three times Oxford returns to his wife, Anne:

Troilus. I am giddy, expectation whirls me round.
   The imaginary relish is so sweet
   That it enchancts my sense. What will it be
   When that the watery palate tastes indeed
   Love's thrice-repured nectar?"

(3.2.17–21)

The following example, Sonnet 107, may be a little more difficult to understand. However, we must remember that Oxford's illegitimate son, the Fair Youth, none other than Southampton, had been confined to the Tower for treasonable acts. The "mortal moon" was Elizabeth. The "eclipse" was a reference to her death. Southampton's life had been forfeited but then changed to imprisonment. When the queen died, James I, who succeeded her, freed Southampton, probably on the recommendation of the earl of Oxford, who by that time was an old man and not far from death.

Not mine own fears, nor the prophetic soul
Of the wide world dreaming on things to come,
Can yet the lease of my true love contol,
Supposed as forfeit to a confined doom.
The mortal moon hath her eclipse endured,
And the sad augurs mock their own presage;
Incertainties now crown themselves assured,
And peace proclaims olives of endless age.
Now with the drops of this most balmy time
My love looks fresh, and Death to me subscribes,
Since, spite of him, Ill live in this poor rime,
While he insults o'er dull and speechless tribes:
And thou in this shalt find thy monument,
When tyrants' crests and tombs of brass are spent.

This is but one example of how Oxford brings his own life into his plays. After a reader experiences score after score of such

personal allusions, how can he fail to see the connection between the earl of Oxford and Shakespeare?

Note the reference to Burghley:

> I seek to heal it only by his wealth.
> Besides these, other bars he lays before me,
> My riots past, my wild societies;
> And tells me 'tis a thing impossible
> I should love thee but as a property.

The remarks of the king in *Hamlet* bear a resemblance to
Elizabeth's resistance to Oxford's desire to travel:

> It is most retrograde to our desire;
> And we beseech you, bend you to remain
> Here in the cheer and comfort of our eye,
> Our chiefest courtier, cousin, and our son.

One cannot really understand Shakespeare without knowing
the full life of Lord Burghley. He had two sons, Thomas and
Robert. Thomas, the older son, was a wayward lad whom Burghley sent to Paris with a governor, Thomas Windebank. Burghley was afraid that Thomas, if he remained at home, would
bring dishonor upon his family. We know he sent him letters and
gave him rules for behavior. These echo the admonishments of
Polonius to Laertos in *Hamlet*:

> Be thou familiar but by no means vulgar. (1.3.65)

> Neither a borrower nor a lender be.
>
> (1.3.79)

Thomas lived it up while in Paris, carousing, wenching, gam-
ing, even stealing. What a cross for his father to bear! No wonder
Burghley put all his efforts into his son Robert.

In reading *Merry Wives of Windsor*, one can realize that Oxford
had married a colorless and childlike Anne. Fenton, of course, is
Oxford.

> *Fenton.* I see I cannot get thy father's love;
>   Therefore, no more turn me to him, sweet Nan.
> *Anne.* Alas! how then?
> *Fenton.* Why, thou must be thyself.
>   He doth object, I am too great of birth
>   And that, my state being gal'd with my expense,
>
> (3.4.1–5)

16
More Examples

All of Shakespeare's plays contain phrases and happenings that touched the life of the earl of Oxford. I shall cite one instance in each of ten plays, although there are many more. Take, for example, *Timon of Athens*. Timon says: "Let my lands be sold." This is exactly what Oxford told Burghley to do when he had to sell some of his estates in order to pay for his trip to Europe in 1575 and 1576.

In *Two Gentlemen of Verona* Valentine kills a man. Oxford had himself killed a cook who, through Burghley's machinations, was spying on him.

In *Titus Andronicus*, Oxford writes, "This monument five hundred years hath stood." He is, of course, reminding the queen of the Vere family's long service to England (1066 to 1562).

In *Antony and Cleopatra*, note the following:

> Royal wench!
> She made great Caesar lay his sword to bed;
> He ploughed her and she cropp'd.
>
> (2.2.231–33)

This was one of the most audacious references Oxford ever made. He was referring to Leicester, a military man who was reputed to be Queen Elizabeth's lover; it was an open secret that she had had a son by him.

This is an example of the great liberties that Oxford took. It would have been impossible for the Stratford Shaksper to be as free as Oxford was. He would surely have had his head chopped off.

In *All's Well That Ends Well*, Bertram says:

> My wife, my liege! I shall beseech your highness
> In such a business give me leave to use the
> help of mine own eyes.
>
> (2.3.109–11)

121

He is, of course, referring to the marriage to Anne Cecil forced upon him by the queen. Oxford pleads for the right to choose his own wife.

In *Measure for Measure*, Oxford talks of usury and "a furred gown to keep him warm." Here he is referring to his father-in-law, who made usury respectable and who usually wore a furred gown. Allusions such as these help us to understand the hatred that Burghley must have had for Oxford and why he and his son Robert were determined to bury the name of Oxford.

In *Twelfth Night*, Sir Andrew says:

> And yet I will not compare with an old man.
>
> (1.3.121)

Oxford and Hatton were rivals for the queen's favor. Oxford is here referring to the fact that Hatton is ten years older than he is. Later on Maria says:

> Marry, Sir, sometimes he is a kind of Puritan.
>
> (2.3.?)

Oxford is again alluding to Hatton, who was a Puritan.

In *Midsummer Night's Dream*, Hermia is talking about herself:

> Because I am so dwarfish and so low?
>
> (3.2.295)

Hermia is really Oxford's wife, Anne, who was both small in person and considered by Oxford to be low in social stature.

In 1579, the French Ambassador Simier was trying to convince Queen Elizabeth to marry Alençon, the French prince. He whispered to the queen that her favorite, Leicester, had secretly married Lettia Knollis. Elizabeth was furious. She also resented the sumptuous gowns the countess of Leicester wore and the luxurious coach she drove around in. Elizabeth's jealously went so far that, in public, she boxed the ears of her rival.

In the second part of *King Henry VI*, the scene is recreated by Oxford, when the queen drops her fan and says:

> Give me my fan; what, minion! can ye not:
> [*Giving the Duchess of Gloucester a box on the ear.*]
> I cry you mercy, madam; was it you?
>
> (1.3.135-36)

In each play there are scores of examples that can be pointed out as having relevance to some part of Oxford's life.

17

Summary

When we study the Stratford Shaksper, we are faced with unexplainable facts that do not jibe at all with the writings of Shakespeare. On the other hand, when we examine the life of Oxford, everything meshes perfectly. The last part of his life—the third period—is a logical and rational development. After his finances had become impossible, he was forced to give up his activity with the theater, the subsidization of a sort of factory of writers. He also did what many men did at the time (and today too): he married for money.

Fortunately, he married a gentle woman of high birth, a lady at court who gave him the peace and solitude he needed at this time of life. The stage plays he had been composing under the grueling pressure of the theater were converted into literature for reading. Thus, starting in 1592 or thereafter, he enjoyed twelve years of peace and uninterrupted work. This period corresponds to the greatest and most mature output of the Shakespearean dramas. The records from 1588 on have disappeared, however. It would almost seem as if some awesome censor had gone to the theaters, to the lord chamberlain's office, to any public office, and had said, "We want all the papers and records pertaining to the earl of Oxford or to Shakespeare." For they have all disappeared.

Do you wonder, then, why some members of the family eventually got together and decided that these priceless works should not be lost to posterity? But they could not get the original manuscripts written in Oxford's neat calligraphy! Isn't that strange? You would think they might have gotten at least one or two. But no, a complete blank.

Now, in the 1592-to-1604 period, there is a flood of works, about two a year. It is not the eight or ten a year knocked out by that miracle man from Stratford, who went from illiteracy in his hometown to overnight production of the greatest English plays in history, or so goes the Stratford myth.

When Oxford died in 1604, as in the case of most writers, some manuscripts were left unfinished.

In 1602, a curious thing happened. The servants of the earl of Oxford and Worcester were given permission to present a play at Boar's Head tavern at Eastcheap, mentioned in *Henry the Fourth, Part I*. It is the only reappearance of Oxford after fourteen years of retirement as a patron of the drama. We don't know what play was presented, because all records of the lord chamberlain have mysteriously disappeared for this year.

There is a connection there with this performance of whatever it was, and it wasn't with Shaksper, it was with Oxford, but it had something to do with Shakespeare's play.

What happened when Oxford died in 1604? Before then, the plays had been coming out under the name of Shakespeare. But after 1604 and for nineteen years following (until the First Folio), nothing more is published with proper authorization. The Shaksper people explain that the Stratford man decided not to write anymore, and to just concentrate on business.

If you wish to pursue this study of the earl of Oxford as the true Shakespeare, my suggestion is to reread the plays of Shakespeare that are particularly autobiographical of the earl. *Hamlet* would come first, *Othello* next, and then *All's Well That Ends Well*. Others might be *Romeo and Juliet*, *The Merchant of Venice*, *Love's Labour's Lost*, and *Taming of the Shrew*.

Looney presents the case for the earl of Oxford very succinctly. What evidence do we have that the earl of Oxford and Shakespeare are one?

1. The poetry he wrote either anonymously or under the signatue, "E.O.", show the same verse forms, ideas and word plays as the Shakespearean verses.
2. The biographical evidence fits exactly into the Shakespearean production.
3. The chronology fits. There is no mystery or need for Procrustean adjustments as in Shaksper.
4. The posthumous evidence also tallies with the issuance or nonissuance of the plays.
5. The autobiographical aspects as evidenced in a number of plays parallel Oxford's life.

It is a pity that we besmirch the most beautiful pages of English cultural development by conforming them to the base intellect and common character of the Stratford person. I hope that we in America, at least, can free ourselves of the vested interests that strangle us and concentrate our future research on the earl of Oxford. In so doing, we shall better appreciate the greatest pages of English literature.

The Elizabethan age was the most active and the most splendid in the history of England, and the man who was a leader in making it possible was the earl of Oxford. This desire for éclat continued under the rule of Elizabeth's successor, James I, except that the disciplined expenditures under the former gave way to wanton excesses and lax control. The days of Elizabeth and Oxford were over. The rising, unbridled extravagance of James I was to lead to the rule of the Puritans.

A Useful Chronological Table

Early Period

1550	Birth of the earl of Oxford.
1558	Elizabeth becomes queen.
1562	Oxford's father dies.
	Oxford becomes ward under guardianship of William Cecil.
	Arthur Golding is hired as private tutor to Oxford.
1571	William Cecil becomes Lord Burghley.
	Oxford marries Anne Cecil.
1573	Oxford tries for naval services. He is refused.
	Oxford sets up a literary workshop in Savoy apartments.
1574.	Oxford runs away to the continent. He is brought back.
1575	Oxford visits Europe.
1576	Oxford returns home.
	Oxford begins separation from his wife. This lasts five years.

Middle Period

1576	Oxford begins his association with writers and actors.
	Oxford starts publication of early lyrics.
1580–84	Oxford's group of players tour the provinces.
	Oxford's secretary, Lyly, becomes his theater manager.
1581	Oxford's son by Anne Vavasor is born.
1584	Oxford's company visits Stratford-on-Avon.
1584–87	In London, Oxford's Boys perform plays written by Oxford, among them *Agamemnon and Ulysses*.

1586	Queen Elizabeth grants Oxford an annuity of one thousand pounds.
1588	The Spanish Armada is defeated
	Oxford's wife dies.
	Oxford begins a life of retirement.

Final Period

1590	Oxford's company of actors is disbanded.
1590	Shaksper's career begins?
1591–92	Oxford marries Elizabeth Trentham.
	Oxford withdraws from public notice.
1593	Oxford's son Henry is born.
1598	The name "Shakespeare" first appears as that of a dramatist
	Shakespearean plays tumble forth until 1604.
1603	Queen Elizabeth dies.
	Oxford officiates at the coronation of James I.
1604	Oxford dies. Well dries up for issuance of plays until *First* Folio.
	Shaksper of Stratford retires?
1616	Shaksper of Stratford dies.
1623	*First Folio* appears.

Helpful Bibliography

This is not a bibliography in the usual sense. It is reading suggested for further study.

The Mysterious Mr. Shakespeare by Charlton Ogburn
  (McLean, Va.: E.P.M. Publishing.)
The Mystery of William Shakespeare by Charlton Ogburn
  (London: Penguin Group, 1988.)

*   *   *   *   *

The next suggestion is in a more unusual form. Judge and Mrs. Miller, in order to make available important Oxfordian texts, have, at their own expense, arranged for the printing and availability of these texts to the general public. They are available from:

> Minos Publishing Company
> P.O. Box 1309
> Jennings, La. 70546
> (telephone: 318-824-4564)

Hidden Allusions in Shakespeare's Plays by Eva Turner Clark
  3d edition, 2 volumes. Edited by Ruth Loyd Miller.
A Hundreth Sundrie Flowres From the Original Edition of 1573
  by Captain Bernard Mordaunt Ward
  2d edition. Edited (and additions) by Ruth Loyd Miller.
Shakespeare Identified in Edward de Vere, Seventeenth Earl of Oxford, and *The Poems of Edward de Vere* by John T. Looney
  3d edition, 2 volumes. Edited by Ruth Loyd Miller.
Also available is a photocopied version of Bernard Mordaunt Ward's *Seventeenth Earl of Oxford*.

*   *   *   *   *

Another book that will interest Oxfordian scholars is:

Shakespeare Revealed in Oxford's Letters by William Plumer Fowler
  (Portsmouth, N.H.: Peter E. Randall.)

*   *   *   *   *

The following book is out of print. It was written by Charlton Ogburn's father and mother. You might be lucky enough to find a copy in a used book depot. I still refer to it.

This Star of England by Dorothy and Charlton Ogburn
  (New York: Coward-McCann, Inc., 1952.)

Index